The spirits have spoken.
Are we ready to listen?

Jeffrey Marks has given us a wonderful tool for demystifying the experience of dying and being conscious in the after-death state. We're coming into a time when we won't necessarily have "the Other Side"—it will be one unified world of energy and consciousness and the "dead" will be as real and easy to communicate with as anyone else. We need clear books like this to understand the continuity of consciousness and how to access the nonphysical dimensions.

— Penney Peirce, author of *Frequency* and *The Intuitive Way*

The evidence for survival of bodily death, from a variety of sources, continues to grow. Jeffrey A. Marks' *The Afterlife Interviews* is a valuable addition, which will fascinate researchers and laypersons alike. Since the likelihood that we shall all die is quite impressive, this book should be of interest to everyone.

— Larry Dossey, MD, author of *Healing Words,*
Reinventing Medicine, and *The Power Of Premonitions*

Jeffrey A. Marks' *The Afterlife Interviews* makes an important contribution to the canon of research in which the nature of human consciousness after physical death is explored through mental mediumship. Marks' repeated findings confirm certain archetypal responses of the souls in Spirit, many of which I recognise from my own work as a medium. I congratulate Jeffrey on undertaking this humbling challenge and for accepting the responsibility to do it so very well. The wisdom, light and love from those on the Other Side shines through these pages, illuminating the minds of everyone who is fortunate to read this important book.

—Michael Wheeler, medium and author of *Heaven Hears Your Heart*
(www.psychicoranges.com, Sydney, Australia)

As a spiritual seeker and medium I am drawn to and relate to *The Afterlife Interviews*. I found it to be wholly enjoyable and enlightening!

— Jodi Livon, The Intuitive Coach and author of *The Happy Medium*

Jeffrey A. Marks has produced a work that any serious student of Spirituality would do well to read again and again.

In a publishing genre where books are bereft of specificity and sorely lacking in detail, he dives right in and tackles the tougher questions of Spirit and conveys answers in a smooth, flowing style that imparts the real intention of the source. So often when the deeper issues are approached in spiritual writing, such questions and difficult answers seem to take leave of the page. Not so with this work.

His work on Time and revelation of knowledge take difficult questions and lay them down in a way that serve not only to enlighten, but also in a way that allows them to be used as tools in the meditation process. Virtually any summary he records from his sessions would make the basis for a good meditation session. In that sense, *The Afterlife Interviews* can be viewed as much as a workbook as a gentle read on a Sunday afternoon.

Information on difficult topics, beautifully imparted, make this a work worth keeping close at hand, and in the toolbox of spiritual practice.

—Bruce W. Holsted, businessman, author of *Sacred Spaces* and
Steps to a Conservation of Mind, and hospice volunteer

As a student of spiritual science (Rudolph's Steiner's Anthroposophy) for twenty-five years, I was very curious about the correspondences I would find between it and Jeffrey Marks' well-done qualitative research in *The Afterlife Interviews*. As a practitioner of energy medicine therapy for thirty years, I was also delighted in the numerous references to the differences in energetic frequencies between life on earth in a physical body and life on the "other side of the threshold," particularly in the dimensions of time, space and matter. Although my Anthroposophy perspective diverges from Jeffrey's regarding simultaneous lifetimes, I was delighted with the numerous other correspondences between Jeffrey's findings and Steiner's spiritual science that felt validated through this fascinating investigation. Finally, I found the author's writing style to be very reader-friendly and understandable. Once I picked up this book, it was difficult to put down. I am grateful for this masterful contribution to expanding our understanding of consciousness, freedom, the divine human journey, life on the other side, and how it all has to do with aligning our thinking, feeling and willing with LOVE.

—Cynthia Hutchison, DNSc, RN, HTCP/I, Director of Healing Touch Program,
and author of *Healing Touch Meditations: Guided Practices
to Awaken Healing Energy for Yourself and Others*

We will all get there someday...
What can we expect?
And what does it mean for us right now?

THE AFTERLIFE
INTERVIEWS

Volume I

Dee -
You are eternal!
Enjoy the journey!

Also by Jeffrey A. Marks:

BOOKS

*Your Magical Soul: How Science and Psychic Phenomena Paint
a New Picture of the Self and Reality*

WEB

Spiritual Exploration and Education (S.E.E.)

www.SpiritualExploration.com

BLOG

*The Inner Voice:
a dialogue on the nature of consciousness,
spirituality, psychic living,
and paranormal science*

http://jeffreymarks.blogspot.com

THE AFTERLIFE
INTERVIEWS
Volume I

Jeffrey A. Marks

Spiritual Medium and Paranormal Researcher

ARAGO PRESS
AN IMPRINT OF ARAGO OMNIMEDIA, LLC

Published in the United States by Arago Press (Lynnwood, Washington)
an imprint of Arago Omnimedia, LLC

Visit us on the Web at www.AragoPress.com

All-around Editor: Heidi Marks
Book design, artwork, and production: Heidi Marks
Cover photo of Face Rock in Bandon, Oregon, and hand illustration ©2012 by Heidi Marks

Publisher's Cataloging-in-Publication Data

Marks, Jeffrey A. (Jeffrey Allan), 1970-
The afterlife interviews, volume I / Jeffrey A. Marks. -- 1st ed. --
Lynnwood, Wash. : Arago Press, c2012.
p. ; cm.
ISBN: 978-1-936492-07-7 (trade paper: acid-free paper)
Summary: Starting with a list of 52 questions regarding the nature of life on the Other Side, the author went directly to the spirits for answers. Volume I covers the first 23 questions: the nature of the dying process itself; the life review; the new spiritual body; new knowledge acquired after passing; how language is facilitated; how spirits exist in the framework of Time; spiritual evolution and levels; reincarnation; the nature of evil; and more. ---Publisher.

1. Future life. 2. Immortality. 3. Death--Psychological aspects. 4. Consciousness. 5. Thanatology. 6. Reincarnation. 7. Mediums. 8. Parapsychology--Research. 9. Spiritualism. I. Title.

BL535 .M37 2012   2012937678
133.9013--dc23   1208

The manufacturer of this book is certified by the Forest Stewardship Council™, Sustainable Forestry Initiative®, and the Programme for Endorsement of Forest Certification™.

FOR MARGO
ALWAYS THE INQUISITIVE ONE

THE LOVE OF FRIENDS AND FAMILY IS FOREVER

"You don't have to be dead to move toward the light."

— Unknown

Volume I

CONTENTS

INTRODUCTION

"Why don't they tell us what life is like on the Other Side?"

It's a question I've heard over and over again, from the curious by-stander to the most skeptical inquirer. In the course of a sitting, when spirits make contact through a medium, we all too often get caught up in the "magic" of the moment—the evidential details that pour out identifying the deceased for which the medium should have no logical way of knowing. Then the emotions also get swept into the event, as it appears the deceased are talking to the sitter from beyond the veil, validating the bonds of the relationships they shared when the spirits were alive here on earth. Perhaps it is because such moments are filled with awe, wonder, and raw emotion that information regarding the nature of the Other Side gets missed. After all, the spirits are really there for the client, placing the focus squarely on him or her, and to reveal that they, as the deceased, are perfectly well and that they still share incredible emotions of love, friend-ship, and in some cases profound forgiveness.

When other mediums have been asked "What do they tell you about the Other Side?" I have been surprised to hear very little. No doubt you have, too. Isn't it a burning curiosity for some of us (if not most of us) to know what life is like after death? Is there such a thing as personal survival and continuity of the soul? Are there any clues that can give us a glimmer of hope that when our final moments on earth disappear we will still abide in some type of environment and not simply vanish into nothingness? Some of the responses to why we have not heard much through the process of mediumship have ranged from: (a) They aren't allowed to talk about it; to (b) It's beyond our comprehension, so words cannot describe it; or (c) It's all love and light and just accept it at that. Option "c" perturbs me the most, because it seems like such a pat answer, spoken without much real thought or investigation into the problem. All three options also don't pan out in regard to the history of mediumship and studies of the afterlife.

As early as 1905, deceased former members of the Society for Psychical Research (SPR) were allegedly coming through mediums being scientifically studied by remaining SPR members, with glimpses of what the nature of the afterlife was like. One of the SPR's founding members, F.W.H. Myers, supposedly wrote an entire book about the Other Side through renowned medium Geraldine Cummins. Of course, one must ask the question, "How do you know it's really the deceased and not just the medium's imagination?" Fair enough. In regard to the Cummins manuscript, several people who were close friends of Myers commented that the concepts and language were very much in style with his thinking and speaking, and the evolution of the spiritual concepts presented would have been a natural progression for him, were he to still be alive. The manuscript spoke so loudly of his personality that Myers' widow offered to make Geraldine a permanent house guest, just so she could feel close to Frederic and perchance have further communication with him.

Emmanuel Swedenborg is widely credited as being the first to document the nature of the Other Side through the concept of mediumship, though he claimed to receive his information directly from God, Christ, and Heavenly angels, rather than deceased people. His encyclopedic collection has been so revered that it was turned into its own structured religion called Swedenborgianism, and his concepts were incorporated into The New Church (General Church of the New Jerusalem.)

Writing between the years of 1758 and 1772, Swedenborg described the Other Side as being in alignment with Scripture, that there was a Heaven and a Hell. He spent the last decades of his life re-interpreting the Bible for its "true" spiritual meaning based on his sense of personal mediumship with the powers of the Divine. The tales surrounding his spiritual journey inspired many mediums in the following centuries. Swedenborg's contribution, while being radical even by today's standards, did ignite certain minds to the possibilities for spiritual connection with the living and was, arguably, the catalyst for starting the movement.

Today, a medium's primary job is not about re-interpreting the Divine, but to provide a much more down-to-earth service: to assist with healing grief. And rightly so. Such phenomena, if it could scientifically be proven real, provides an extraordinary way of extinguishing the sense of loss a person feels at the passing of a loved one. To date, there are a few institutions whose sole objective is to study such phenomena and bring to light the veracity of the claims. The results from some of these have been incredibly tantalizing. But when it comes to the research of mediums and mediumship, the scientists can only use the criteria of what can be considered evidential: names, dates, physical descriptions, recalled events the psychic would not know about, or other information which required some research (such as the deceased saying "I left a copy of my will in the left drawer of my desk, yet to be found" and then having someone follow up and actually find the document). This kind of research doesn't allow for speculation; hence it would not be suitable to ask in an exploratory setting regarding "What is the nature of the Other Side like?" You would not be able to validate the answer.

That doesn't mean an answer isn't forthcoming, or that it isn't relevant. At the very least, an answer—though unable to be scientifically proven—does provide *possibilities*. This was the approach I took when I began studying the nature of paranormal phenomena when I joined the Washington State Ghost Society. After I heard my first clear EVP (electronic voice phenomena) of a spirit speaking into my audio recorder's microphone, my curiosity lit like gasoline on a fire. BOOM! I thought to myself, "Here's an opportunity to learn something about the nature of consciousness!" Though my findings probably wouldn't stand up to rigid scientific scrutiny (oftentimes presenting more questions than answers), at the very least what I might learn could present possibilities, where before there had been none. I devised a list of twenty-two questions about what life was like as a ghost and started asking them at every investigation hoping that I would get answers in the form of an EVP.

I have observed that the history of ghost research has always been wrought with the simple question "Why?" But to me, it needed to go a bit further. Not only the "why," but to ask from the ghost's own point of view, "what is a spirit's life like?" It was a perspective no one had really taken before, at least not to my knowledge. Some of the questions I asked were: "Do you still perceive the movement of time?"; "Do you notice a tunnel of light following you?"; "Do you ever get hungry?"; "Do you sleep or are you always awake?" Despite what some in the spiritual/metaphysical community have said, there are spirits who are willing to talk about the nature of the afterlife. Not every question I have asked has received an answer, but a good many of them have. And indeed, those answers suggest possibilities inherent in the nature of consciousness.

So when I kept hearing that single all-important critique of modern mediums—"Why don't they tell us what the Other Side is like?"—I knew from my research at haunted locations asking EVP questions to ghosts (who are existing "in-between" our world and the Other Side), that I could do the same for spirits who had crossed "through the light" all the way over to the Other Side. Why not? I have been a practicing medium for over a decade. Perhaps the reason other mediums have not gotten answers is because they're too focused on assisting their client, who can admittedly get caught up in the moment of communication, or they don't believe they can get sensible answers. My thought has been, maybe they just haven't asked the right questions or were not willing to entertain the possibilities. Since ghosts at haunted locations have been willing to answer my EVP questions on occasion, I was willing to gamble that a person's deceased relative who has passed all the way to the Other Side would be willing to do the same. Why not? Wouldn't you want to tell your long-lost son or beloved daughter back on earth what a wonderful life awaits them? Or just how grand you really are doing living on the Other Side? At the very least, wouldn't you want to offer a sense of possibilities to the rest of humanity?

That's what this is about. Possibilities. No, we cannot validate with any sense of certainty the nature of the Other Side, but I think we can accept the idea of possibilities. It's the same with the process of mediumship itself. No, scientists have not been able to validate with certainty a deceased loved one is communicating, but the possibility is really there, based on the statistical hits. It's not that much different than scientists believing theories for which they currently have no physical evidence to support them, such as string theory or wormholes or parallel dimensions. Mathematically they appear plausible, but there is no real evidence. For mediumship, we have excellent circumstantial evidence; it is just that science hasn't yet been able to come up with the "how" or "why" it works—the mathematics of it. For me, having done this for over a decade, my point of view will obviously be slanted—I do believe I am receiving information from deceased people. The feelings that overcome my body, the images that speak of veridical information and that have been verified by my clients, are not a matter of speculation in my consciousness: they are established fact. And I understand, for some people, that's just my opinion and they will never accept such philosophy and may certainly try their damnedest to deny it. That's fine. I'm not here to convince skeptics or change people's minds. I only wish to present *possibilities*.

What do these possibilities present?

A view, as we have never been offered before, on the nature of surviving death and what awaits us—straight from the mouths of those who are there. (For the skeptics or sideliners, I'll just say "*potentially* straight from the mouths...") What I have compiled in this volume isn't "divine inspiration" handed down from an archaic tradition or belief system which requires an allegiance of faith; this is a modern-day inquiry using tools and techniques which have actually been with us since history began, but for whatever reason have been feared, ignored, or gone undeveloped by the mass populace due to misunderstanding and social biases. Today, these processes are being carefully studied, with some scientists already firmly in the camp of acknowledging the real possibility of the information coming from the deceased. It's my desire to take this possibility and employ it to the betterment and evolution of my fellow human beings. Remember, I'm just presenting *possibilities*. To help ease the fear of death would a tremendous gift for us all. It's my goal that my work with *Th* *Interviews* passes that onto you.

Now let's get on with how this project was constr and its ultimate outcome.

THE SET UP

In order to get a large enough pool of information in which to draw conclusions, I decided upon doing fourteen individual sittings. Why fourteen? For several reasons—but time and availability, mainly. The Interviews lasted on average two to three hours each, then I had to transcribe each conversation that I had recorded. Each Interview, when completed, accounted for a huge chunk of time—sometimes hard to slip in while working a full-time "regular" job, handling individual sittings, group sessions, public presentations, and other paranormal research I was committed to, not to mention also just living life.

The other reason I decided to stop with the fourteenth sitting was because by the tenth Interview, I was noticing similarities in the answers. This is not to suggest that I was pulling up what had already been spoken before, but rather that the spirits had already divulged enough information and were starting to say relatively the same thing with only minor differences, adding their own unique personal slant to it, as we are all apt to do when describing things. The answers weren't identical, by no means, but when I started looking back at the culmination of responses to individual questions, I was seeing the pattern that was emerging—the overall gestalt of information that was being presented. It was at that point that I decided to stop at fourteen (considering all the other projects I was committed to), tally it all up, and present it. If all fourteen were saying relatively the same thing with only minor personal colorations and differences based on their experiences, then I must take on faith as valid the overall answers the group had given in response to the questions.

At the start of each session, I would "tune in" and reveal what information I felt I was receiving from the sitter's deceased friend or relative in order to verify that I was linked with the spirit—such as medical conditions, how the spirit passed, dates, other events, names, and personality traits. After sufficient validation on at least eight to ten data points (and in most cases, many more), and when my sitter and I were confident that a connection was happening, I would have the sitter ask a pre-determined set of fifty-two questions regarding the nature of the dying process and ‑hat life was like on the Other Side. The actual Interview, as mentioned ‑ve, lasted on average of about two to three hours, although a few sittings went significantly longer. The Interview was recorded on my digital audio recorder and transcribed later into a spreadsheet with each question designated on its own tab in the workbook. Once the fourteen sittings had been recorded and transcribed, I returned to each question individually and examined the fourteen separate answers collectively to gain an overall response to the question. As you'll see, I have pulled out particular passages as they were revealed in the sessions to demonstrate the nature of the answers and how I formulated my interpretations.

THE CHALLENGES TO THIS RESEARCH
AND HOW I DEALT WITH THEM

CHALLENGE 1.
Handling the project and data all on my own.

When I originally conceived this mission, I had intended to enlist the assistance of a second medium and do it as a blind experiment. The hope was that between two mediums, if both of us connected with the same deceased individuals we would theoretically receive the same type of answers. To keep it blind, the mediums would not share their responses (or even who they connected with) until after the sittings had been concluded to see if things matched up. Unfortunately, I got too consumed with wanting to get the project underway, plus I did not have access to a notable second medium in my particular geographical area when I started the project (at least none that I was aware of at the time, although a few have come to my attention since then), nor was I interested in coordinating the schedules of *three* people for each Interview times fourteen. I knew that in the end, no matter whether a second medium had come aboard and we had received positive statistical results regarding (a) validation of possible communication with a sitter's deceased friend or relative, and (b) similar responses from such individuals to each of the fifty-two questions, the skeptics and non-believers would most likely still remain skeptics and non-believers. Ultimately, whether alone or in tandem with a second medium, the information can only be presented as a possibility regarding the nature of the Other Side and not scientific fact.

Would a second medium provide additional "weight" to the material and make it more credible? Sure. And to that, I would challenge the plethora of mediums in the world to begin conducting their own versions of "afterlife interviews" and see what they receive. And I would certainly be open to conducting a similar process again through the blind standards I originally intended to conduct. However, after looking over the data, I am satisfied with the results that each Interview was answered by an individual in spirit connected to the sitter. On one occasion, the sitter told me she had asked many of the same questions of her deceased brother when she met him in an out-of-body experience after he died, and the answers he gave me were the same as he had told her during that encounter. Additionally, I sometimes draw the images I receive and show them to my client, and she confirmed that my drawings were nearly identical to the images he had given her. In the end, not having the second medium in my opinion doesn't make the information any less valid or valuable.

CHALLENGE 2.
Distortions in the "psychic signal" can affect the responses to the questions.

To be blunt, no psychic is ever 100% accurate 100% of the time. Distortions in imagery, sound, and feelings can result in erroneous interpretations—and sometimes the psychic can just be plain wrong. It was for this reason that I chose to do multiple sittings. Statistically speaking, one sitting may not necessarily be as "strong" as another, and having fourteen to work from provided a pool that could "smooth out" the peaks and the valleys and still give a fairly "workable" idea as to the answer of each question. I created a spreadsheet of what I documented related to the personal validations of the deceased for each sitter, showing both the "hits" and the "misses." This ratio of hits to misses could be taken as a possible sense of "strength" for how that particular Interview session could be regarded. Since I am presenting the material from the standpoint of strictly being "possibilities," I feel the hits strongly outweigh the misses, to the tune of 85 – 90%, and I am fine with that. From where I sit, if we had even a 15 – 20% greater idea as to the nature of what the afterlife could potentially be, think of how much impact that could have on our collective lives here on earth. Though I feel the personal validation items fall into the higher percentage range for accuracy, some people may wish to argue semantics with that notion and may not be comfortable applying that same percentage to the answers I received for the questions. That's fine. To each his own. Hence the reason for fourteen sittings to balance things out.

CHALLENGE 3.
Is it all in my imagination and I am simply repeating myself?

This was a legitimate concern before I conducted the very first Interview. As to whether or not it was my imagination, I trusted my consciousness to the same energy that had to first validate its presence as a deceased friend or relative of the sitter by providing multiple data points for evidential reference. Every spirit has a unique feeling to them and along with that feeling comes nuances in personality, tone, and style of response. What I soon discovered was that these nuances found their way into the responses of the questions. What's more, on several occasions, the deceased would forego answering a question until they had an opportunity to throw out another personal validation to reveal we were still "in sync."

My greatest concern was "Am I simply repeating what another spirit had already told me?" Again, I relied on my connection to the individual personality and its unique style and feeling to provide the answers. When I felt that certain answers were too identical to the style and response of a previous spirit, I would take a moment to relax, clear my mind, and connect up again to see if I got hit with the same response. This pause didn't happen often, but sometimes it did.

There was also concern for preconceived notions. I formulated the fifty-two questions myself and it would be absurd to say I had no idea what their responses *might* be. When you work with spirits for over a decade, though they may not directly tell you what's going on with them on the Other Side, you do get a sense of what things might be like, and so that does present the possibility of the medium's mind superimposing an answer over the spirit's real declaration. To that end, I can only offer that I approached each Interview as a curiosity seeker; that each Interview was perceived as a separate and unique event, and that I was not interested in coming up with my own answers. If I had wanted to promote my own answers, I wouldn't have bothered wasting hundreds of hours interviewing and typing out the responses—I could have done five Interviews, called it great, and closed that portion to begin writing the book. Incidentally, I did come in with thoughts of what I felt certain answers might be; yet what I received from some spirits was the exact opposite of my expectations. That was excellent—for it showed me the answers weren't coming from my own mind.

CHALLENGE 4.
Could it be ESP with the sitter?

This is a standard concern, whether doing an Afterlife Interview or a normal sitting. Could the information the medium receives be simply ESP with the client? It's a legitimate question. However, after pouring over the answers to the fifty-two questions, it became clear early on that the sitters were not thinking the types of responses I received. For many, they had no clue themselves as to how to answer a majority of the questions and were just as curious as I was in hearing what their deceased friends or relatives had to say. On many occasions the sitters often replied, "That's fascinating. I never would have thought of that myself." Again, since my focus is on the feeling of the energy of the spirit and what it reveals to me, I do not believe the responses were a result of ESP with my sitters.

CHALLENGE 5.
Obtain various multi-cultural backgrounds for comparison.

One of the things that really excited me about this project was the chance to interact with those of different faiths in order to get a variety of perceptions. Does someone from the Islamic faith have a different experience of the afterlife versus a Christian or a Buddhist? What didn't occur to me was that some faiths don't look too highly on people who claim to receive information from the dead; or that sitters of different ethno-religious backgrounds already have a firm belief on what the nature of the afterlife is like based on their ancient religious texts and aren't willing to hear other possibilities. Alas, the multicultural aspect of the Interviews turned out not to be as great as I had hoped. I did achieve connecting with three deceased relatives from the Islamic faith; one Hindu; one primarily Jewish; several Christians; and the rest falling under either agnostic or non-believers while they were on earth. Though I would have liked more participants in terms of a multicultural background, the answers received from the few who did participate reflected similarly with what everyone else in the majority was telling me. At this point, I take on faith that the experience of everyone—regardless of philosophical upbringing—is similar and not that one faith experiences anything truly different from another.

OVERALL CONCLUSIONS AND PERSONAL OBSERVATIONS

There are very few events that act as cornerstones on one's journey through life. For most people, only one or two things truly qualify—the birth of a child, winning the lottery, or that sort of thing. And those events qualify because they converge on the person's character, perceptions, and way of being. Indeed, the events are *life changing* in every respect. When I finished my first Interview in this project, I knew this was going to be the case with the entire material in my life. After my first Interview ended and my client left the house, I was so stunned and literally dumbfounded, I sat on the floor for nearly an hour and just gazed into empty space. I was so humbled by the experience that I couldn't remain standing. I had fifty-two questions answered, with excellent imagery and impression, and combined with the evidential material to support communicating with the deceased—it was one of the most profound moments of my life. I knew by the end, after soaking in fourteen Interviews, it was going to change me irrevocably, and it has.

What's more, I received more than just the psychic responses.

Since I recorded each session with my digital audio recorder that I take on paranormal investigations, it came as no surprise that I would capture EVPs as well. On several occasions, the voices of the deceased found their way into the audio, oftentimes confirming what I was psychically receiving and reporting to the sitter. None of the EVPs I received contradicted what I had to say, and in one case, what I reported was exactly what the spirit spoke into my recorder before I said it. Since you can't hear EVPs at the time of the recording and only when you listen back to the audio later, to hear the spirit say two phrases and then have me repeat them as a psychic impression is truly an amazing occurrence. EVPs didn't appear in every Interview, but nevertheless, they did show up in quite a few. I also noticed during times of transcription, I would catch shadows briefly zipping behind me in the reflection of the window in front of me. There were also occasions of flashing lights bursting in the room. This was the spirits' way of informing me just how valid and valuable the project was in completing.

PROCESSES & COMMUNICATIVE TEXT STYLE
AS TRANSCRIBED IN THE BOOK

It's important for the reader to know *how* my style of mediumship works, so as to have a better understanding of the answers as they have been transcribed in the text. A lot of people envision a spirit leaning into the medium's ear and speaking what they want to say. Sadly, this is not how most medium's work (there are a few that do, but I'm not one of them). I receive information from spirits in a combination of ways, usually all happening at once. I will see images in my mind's eye, feel impressions inside and outside of my body, and occasionally hear a word or two tossed about within the mix. This combination informs me of the message the deceased wishes to impart.

In the transcriptions of the audio recordings of the sittings—which are inset (in a different font) as block text throughout the main narrative—you will see both my psychic impressions (including fragmented thoughts and not-so-perfect grammar), and also quotes from the spirit as if he or she were speaking to me. "She says, '*They took me down the hall and showed me a golden statue.*'" I have placed the spirit's message in quotes and italicized it, as if it were actual dialogue I was hearing. This was really not the case, but because of the combination of imagery, feeling, or words I was receiving, this indeed was the information they were imparting, and therefore easier to report in this manner of style. In some cases, short phrases or single words were directly heard by my senses or were visually spelled out in front of me, which taken in combination with the other impressions, definitely needed to be reported in this manner. So keep in mind, when I quote the words of a spirit, it is not because they were standing beside me speaking in my ear; it was because the intensity of the images they were giving me, the feelings they were imparting to me, and the phrases or words they were speaking or writing before my mind's eye, all combined to create the message—and it was done with such energy and force that they might as well had been speaking it with physical vocal chords and mouth. On a few occasions, they did speak into my microphone, resulting in EVPs which corroborated the messages I was verbalizing for them.

THE MULTIPLE VOLUME APPROACH (VOLUME I)

It was decided that because the amount of information received for all fifty-two questions was so vast, it would have been too expensive (and bulky) to create as a single book, hence the need for two volumes. Additionally, the questions cover a huge range—from the dying process all the way to the nature of evil, governance, and philosophy on the Other Side—thus it made sense to break it up. Volume I really sets the stage, giving us a glimpse of what we go through as we leave the body and begin life on the Other Side. Volume II goes deeper into the landscape, lifestyles of the deceased, and philosophical viewpoints on the nature of creation, God, et cetera. Needless to say, these first two volumes presented even more questions, so now I am considering another round of Interviews for a third volume. To that, I will simply say, "To be continued…"

—Jeffrey A. Marks
Seattle, Washington
Planet Earth
2012

Was the Process of Leaving the Body—Dying—a Painful One? What Was It Like for You?

The thought of death has got to be one of mankind's greatest fears—if not the biggest of them all. For so many, it provides the terror of annihilation and the end of days. The fear of losing one's self, all that has been learned, experienced, and the leaving behind of friends and family. When the specter of death comes calling, a whole plethora of thoughts and emotions rise up within one's consciousness. Let's face it, dying in the western world has a lot of stigma attached to it. For the medical profession, death is tantamount to ultimate failure when caring for a patient. The only potential solace one has when considering leaving this world is what a religion or other belief system tells us—and then, when facing that moment head-on, how much comfort do those beliefs really bring?

Since the thought of dying is such a feared moment in our culture, it was my intention to begin *The Afterlife Interviews* from that fateful ending here on earth and follow each soul through his or her progression on the Other Side, as he or she experienced it (and were willing to talk about it). Though physical life might have ended here, the process of dying heralded a new life over there. I wanted to find out just how this transition was handled by those spirits coming through in each sitting. Would the answer ease our own personal fears when it comes time to face our own demise?

By the time this first question was asked, both I and my sitter were already confident that a deceased friend or relative had appeared by the nature of evidential detail supplied at the start of the Interview session. Such things as medical conditions or the nature of the relationship—mother, father, brother, sister, husband, or friend—had been established. Additionally, personal characteristics, names or initials, significant dates, and other notable personal events had been confirmed. Quite frankly, I wasn't willing to begin asking the questions without such data. What use would it be to carry on such a lengthy interview if we weren't even comfortable that a connection was even made? (Incidentally, two Interviews did not even make it to the first question because I was not comfortable with the quality of connection. However, these were exceptions and not the rule). In some cases, as many as fifteen or sixteen pieces of detail were given before remembering what my sitter and I had come together to do, as we had gotten so caught up in the personal communications happening!

Of course, in asking "What was the process of dying like for you?" you're going to get unique qualities and stories from person to person. These details provided another layer of confirmation that a connection to the deceased was occurring, such as with the grandmother of my fourth sitter, Grace. She has since become a good friend, but at the time of the session had no idea what a medium was, yet was open to the possibility of some kind of process whereby the consciousness of her grandmother could be picked up and understood, if only on a basic intuitive level. She was very close to her grandmother, and to be witness for what the process actually revealed was an amazing experience for her. What follows is a short transcription as it was recorded from the session:

> She goes back to the brain thing...Was there a bursting? I see and hear "Whoosh!" When this happened, it wasn't long after that. It was quick. And she was lying down at the time.

Indeed, there had been a bursting, just as I had received. As mentioned above, before asking this question, other details had already come through for Grace to show that her grandmother was making a connection—and to have her provide this answer in response to her own death further cemented that reality for my friend. In another case, a young man named Brandon was coming through for my second sitter, Jodi. The image he kept showing me was his hand on a gun, telling me he had shot himself.

As would happen when it came to the deceased describing the end of their lives, they often mentioned they had a long-standing illness that finally took its course, or that something happened rather suddenly, such as a heart attack or being murdered. In all cases, in regard to this initial question, the spirits related the same thing: *any physical pain vanishes at the moment of death.* In a couple of cases, this was the most startling detail that signaled to the spirit that they had died, as they had become so used to feeling physical pain from having lived with it so long in the body. As mentioned in the tenth session, my sitter, Marti, who conducted the session by phone, was listening again to her mother who had passed away into spirit. This is what Marti's mother was showing me and how I reported it:

> She was caught up in the pain towards the end...She was so caught up in the energy of the pain in her body...The pain didn't carry over, but the wave of energy she was holding on to did when she went. It was like this big energetic charge. But she says, "*Painful, no, but a buzzing feeling.*"

For my friend Grace, it wasn't the absence of pain which told her grandmother she had passed, but the sudden sense of feeling that swept through her—sensations she had lost due to her condition. This is how I described it during the session:

> She's saying for at least a year or more prior to this, she had no energy. Her body felt heavy; weighted down. I would characterize it as being numb, as if the nerves provided no feeling. When she died, all feeling went "whoosh" right back into her. She says, "*When that happened, I felt more alive than I have in a couple of years.*"

For my second sitting in this series, a young boy named Brandon had committed suicide by shooting himself (I mentioned earlier that he had showed me the gun). One question we always ask in hearing of these tragic cases is how can someone go through with it? How does one go through the process of taking his or her own life? In this particular instance, Brandon had found a way to disassociate his mind from the act itself, allowing him to go through with the deed. This is how I described it in the session:

> He does not put himself in the moment; he puts himself out-side of it. He says the only way he could have gotten through it was to disassociate himself from performing the action. He says when he finally *"woke up"*—that's how he wants to say it—as soon as he gave himself conscious permission to view, he noticed he still had this...

I pounded my chest, giving recognition to still having life and a form. Brandon continued feeding me information:

> He says, *"You don't know what it's like seeing yourself standing up when you are expecting to see yourself lying on the floor."* He has no description, no recollection, of the moment of passing. It's as if to say, *"I never even pulled the trigger."*

For all my sitters, the biggest hurdle to dying expressed by those on the Other Side wasn't the moment of death itself, but rather, it was learning to let go of all the emotion, fear, and resistance surrounding the departure into that unknown. Many spirits talked about clinging to this side; really trying to hang on. But when the actual moment of leaving the body occurred, there was no sensation of pain whatsoever. From session eight, my sitter, who went by the initials M.G., was hearing again from the spirit of her mother:

> She actually hung on towards the end there, is that correct?

M.G. confirmed that indeed, her mother did resist – unwilling to let go of life on earth. Her mother continued:

> She shows me going to an end point, but not jumping off the diving board. There was some apprehension about going. She gets right up to the end...*"I get on the diving board, and*

I'm hanging on and hanging on." And then she puts a little blip right before the jumping off point, as if to say, *"Somebody thought I was already dead but wasn't."* She makes me feel like, leaving the body was rather…lots of energy. It wasn't painful, it was charged. It was a "charged" energetic exit.

For a few clients, their beloved relative had been so drugged up on pain killers, they actually left the body earlier than what the doctors had recorded in their logs, as was the case with my eleventh sitter, Terri, who was hearing from her recently departed grandmother, Rose:

She says, *"I went before the morphine even took me,"* making me feel like, even though she was out and the doctors were still declaring her alive, she really had already gone—her body was the only thing that was working; her consciousness (spirit) had already departed. She is claiming to have left before the body went down.

For my twelfth sitter, Kourtnie, the spirit of her father related this information to me:

The process is very easy. He was really drugged up and alone at the time of death. The drugs made him feel like he couldn't even be a part of the body.

It was apparent from the composite of the sittings that departing the physical body is actually quite easy at the moment of death. Several talked about how—when they finally accepted they were dying—they simply flopped out of the body, essentially stepping out of it like a pair of clothes. From my third session, Nancy, my sitter, was hearing from her deceased father. He said it so simply when it came to leaving the body: "I slip out." Grace's grandmother, from my fourth session, informed me that as soon as she acknowledged "I let go," she did a back-flip out of her body.

For my eighth sitter, M.G., her mother passed from a brain tumor and was having cognitive trouble near the end. For her, death brought her back to clarity. This is what her mother was showing, as transcribed from the session:

> She was mentally battling holding on…She shows me flipping
> out backwards. She flipped out backwards and felt, *"As soon
> as I'm out, everything cleared up. It was like the clouds parted
> and I had total awareness."*

The act of departure can become an incredibly emotional time, especially for the deceased. This was brought home by the spirit of my fourteenth sitting. The deceased, Diane, had passed from cancer a year earlier and was a friend of my wife, Heidi, who was the sitter for this session. While alive, Diane led a somewhat isolated life—her family was out of state and she had never married—items which came up during the initial connection stage of the sitting determining whether or not she was communicating. What she was showing me in answer to this question about the dying process was how she had lain in bed contemplating her final moments…and how they left her feeling sullen. This is how it came out in the session:

> She was alone at the time. She makes me feel alone. The closer
> she got, the more unhappy she became. It was emotional. I
> think that's because…she realized she didn't have strong
> connections to other people. That sense of family feeling
> wasn't there. It's like, *"Who's going to celebrate my life?"* I
> think she…her ego was there. *"Who's going to celebrate me?*
> *Nobody around to do that."* As far as the transition, that was
> nothing. But it was an emotional passing. *"Where's the horn*
> *that's going to toot for me?"*

From these loved ones, their message regarding the process of dying was clear: when it comes time to leave the body, there is no physical pain. It is a natural transition—though it may startle you when it occurs. Sometimes we do cling to our life on earth, afraid to let it go, but once we release our fear, we slip out from the decaying flesh into the light of a new world with incredible ease.

Did You Enter a Tunnel of Light or Did You Remain Behind? What Happened Next?

Anyone familiar with the literature and stories of Near Death Experiences (NDEs) has heard of people leaving their body and entering a tunnel, zooming toward a brilliant light. Though this is a common occurrence with NDEs, I was curious if it was natural at the real moment of death—that is, when it's known you're not coming back.

The other reason I asked about the tunnel was because of my research with the Washington State Ghost Society. One of my Electronic Voice Phenomena (EVP) questions I ask of an earthbound spirit is "Are you aware of a tunnel of light following you?" I have heard on some occasions that this tunnel is always present around everyone, as if to say everyone has their own personal vacuum tube hovering nearby to swallow them up and transport them to the Other Side. One ghost responded audibly on my recorder with a sense of surprise, "You know about the tunnel of light?"

When it came to the answers I received in the Interviews, I was surprised, yet still mystified by the tunnel. For some, it was there right away. For others, either they failed to see it or chose not to enter it immediately—and it was apparent they had their reasons, as was the case with my first sitter, Leah, whose friend Michael had passed as the result of possible murder. (The case of his death was never solved—it could have been murder, or potentially suicide. The spirit had shown me the image of a bloody knife, which is my symbol for dying at the hands of another person.) This is how I explained Michael's encounter with the light to Leah:

He remained a little bit. The tunnel of light was an experience he wasn't ready for...What happened next? He was stunned. This is not a passing that was expected. He says, "*It throws you for a loop. Though you might have ideas and perceptions of what the afterlife is like, when you finally get there, it's like... Yeah, it's real...but it still throws you for a loop. You go, 'Oh my God, is this really happening?'*"

In the case of my second sitter, the spirit of Brandon who had committed suicide, the realization that he had continued on was expectedly traumatic. It was equally heart-wrenching when connecting with him about it:

He screamed...I can hear him screaming. His scream has nothing to do with the guilt of leaving people behind...It has everything to do with "*Oh my God, I'm still going on.*" And yes, he says the light was right there. It came to him. And he is going, "*Oh my God, oh my God, oh my God.*" The experience was traumatic in the sense that things started happening very quickly... He did not know what was going on from second to second. He says he was looking for peace and when he hit the Other Side, things were happening so quickly...It turned out not to be the peace he was hoping to achieve.

For Brandon to enter the light, he needed to master the courage to face whatever his potential future might be. He did this by holding on to the memory of my sitter's daughter, who had often helped him during trying times in his life. I asked Jodi if Brandon had a connection to her daughter, and she confirmed he had. At that point, I would not allow her to elaborate on the nature of their relationship, in case more information was forthcoming. After the sitting, Jodi was able to confirm what Brandon had said in the interview:

He's making me feel like...she was one of the people trying to help him. He takes her energy and places it over himself. I don't know if he was calling out to her or asking for some kind of strength because of the nature of their relationship. But then he says he was engulfed by the light; he was swallowed up by it.

For others, once they realized they had left the body and were all right, their attention returned back to their family before moving forward. From session seven, where my sitter, Debbie, was hearing from her father:

> I keep hearing *"No, no, no,"* as if to say he wasn't ready to go yet. There's a reference to making sure you got home okay... *"When I saw the light there, I knew...my life now was going to be different. With the light there, I wanted to make sure the two of you* [Debbie and her mother] *got home okay."* But he still...was not ready to let go.

From session ten, as I related the information from the spirit of Marti's mother:

> She didn't enter the light right away...For one, she was a little dazed from the experience of dying. Then there's mention of the kids. There is this hole where the kids would be...She hesitated for a day or two before entering the light...It's like *"unfinished business."* She says at that point, a relative came from the light and said it was time to go.

From session eleven, with Terri's grandmother, Rose:

> She says, *"Oh, I remained behind a little bit because I wanted to peek in on everybody. I wanted to see how everybody was doing."* Then she says, *"I had people waiting there for me to go down the tunnel and I kind of held them off...in order to see the people here one last time."*

Then there were those who zoomed down the tunnel right away, as if there were no chance to look back. From session three, with the spirit of Nancy's father:

The moment of death was like a blackout and all of a sudden there was this light. It wasn't until he saw that light did he realize he had actually died…He says, *"It came right away."*

From session four, with the spirit of Grace's grandmother:

She says the tunnel of light came very quickly. She says it was open and just sucked her in…She says, *"I didn't quite understand what was happening…Things were just going and going."*

For Diane in my fourteenth sitting, the prospect of dying lonely was soon abated by the appearance of two relatives. Seeing them reassured her that she was being celebrated:

She makes me feel like she was met by two relatives. There was a brother…Feels brother. Then along with a second person, which she's not giving me details, but there are two; they were there to greet her when she finally slipped out of the body. She pretty much went into the light right away due to that emotion about "who's going to celebrate me?" They bring her the celebration. They gave her some heart stuff. And she was like, *"Let's get out of here and go!"*

The moment of death, no doubt, can present a combination of both fear and confusion, no matter what our beliefs of the afterlife might have been while we were alive. It's one thing to theorize and philosophize and believe mentally in an afterlife, but when one is actively engaged in the journey into that sphere, a whole slew of emotions and thoughts can come flooding in, as now the afterlife experience is real and not just imaginary. And sometimes our earthly expectations don't necessarily mesh with the actual occurrence, as it did for the father of Cynthia, the spirit from my fifth session:

He did not enter the tunnel right away. *"Confusion"* is the word…It's like he's standing there going, *"What just happened?"* and then trying to get a bearing…It took him awhile to figure out that he was not considered "alive" anymore. I don't know what his spiritual beliefs were…but he's making me feel like, *"What I believed before and what I encountered afterward did not mesh—So I stood there saying, 'This isn't happening…This isn't happening.'"*

For some, the tunnel didn't appear, but rather a mist. My sixth sitter, Sarah, whose grandfather was a devout Muslim, related his moments just following the exit of his body in the following fashion:

He says he got down on his knees. The feeling he's giving me… *"I knew life was done here; I needed to prepare."* So getting down on his knees was his act of preparation—prayer…*"Then I was approached by three people. Two of them were family members."* He claims one of them as a brother. The other is also a sibling, but he's not giving me brother or sister, just that the other is also related. The third one is not somebody he knew, but who was referenced to be like an angel. They put a hand on his shoulder and said, *"It's okay, stand up, and the angel here, is here…It's okay, you're going to be okay."*

He didn't perceive it as quite a tunnel of light…He's showing it to me like a white mist that just kind of started opening up in front of him and surrounding him. He didn't feel necessarily like he was shooting down a tunnel, but there was this mist that opened up and wrapped around him. He got really scared when that started happening…He's saying, *"You don't know what is going to happen next…"*

He's making me feel—and what he's showing me—he was so shocked at seeing himself and realizing he was dead, and then seeing his brother and then this happening…His mind could not fall into sync…It was happening too quickly. He couldn't easily grasp what was going on. He's also making me feel like…Okay, we have this process and idea of what we think dying is supposed to be like…But his perspective from going through it…*"Okay, I'm going through the process now;*

I've got to let it be what it is, whether it coincides with what we've been taught or not; it is what it is and I have to let it be that way, because it is God's will—it's not necessarily mine or anybody else's." He pretty much let any preconceived ideas in his head go out the door, to let it just happen.

He's making me feel like, it was nice to have the brother there and the other person there…His trust was more in them than the angel figure…He had never seen this other being before. They may call it an angel, but he doesn't recognize it that way; it was an unknown person. So his trust and faith was in people he *did* know. He latched onto that when this mist enveloped him.

For my thirteenth sitter, Gabi, it came out that the mist was the perfect step in moving forward for the spirit of her mother, as her mother reported to me that she "didn't like speed; didn't like to go fast." When I mentioned this, Gabi exclaimed, "She hated going fast! She was the slowest driver on the road!" Her mother continued, as transcribed from the session:

"I did not do the tunnel thing—they knew I wouldn't like the tunnel thing. I got the mist thing." She's telling me, *"Tunnel would be too fast for me."* You know how, when people describe it, they describe it as being sucked down a tube?

Gabi interjected, "That would have terrified her." I kept going, as the information was coming quickly:

She agrees, saying, *"I had the mist, because I would have been too scared."* She's making me feel like, when the mist came over, it was very comforting and relaxed her even further. She says, *"Now I'm dead on earth but alive here…But you don't know what's going to happen next."* So when this mist started forming, there was some kind of recognition…Somehow she knew she was going to be all right. When it took over…It started speeding her up. She could feel herself changing, but not the stuff around her.

Zooming through a tunnel and diving into light or being surrounded by mist does appear to be universal, although the timing of moving into that space appears to be individualistic and not necessarily predetermined. From my ghost research, I have heard some cultures believe a person hangs around for a certain number of days—almost ritualistically or dogmatically—before fully crossing. I'd have to say, at this point, such philosophy might be in error and the truth of the matter may be more accountable to an individual's personal experience rather than theological philosophy.

But the light is always there when one is ready, as revealed by the spirits.

Did You Meet a Spiritual Teacher, Guide, Relative, or Religious Figure?

People who work in hospice often speak of the dying mentioning they are in the presence of deceased friends and relatives before passing. In the western world, most of these occurrences are attributed to hallucinations from drugs or the brain creating figments of the imagination. Yet there are cases where the patients were neither drugged nor losing their minds—it was simply a matter-of-fact statement that "my dead relatives are here." It is logical to assume that such assistance from someone who has gone on before us would be there to ease the transition. Indeed, such was the case in all my sessions—each person was met by someone. I wished to know who that someone was, and if the deceased could shed newfound light on such things as spirit guides and/or religious icons.

As one would expect, already deceased relatives would be the best way to facilitate the transition. It is far easier to relax and trust someone you know rather than someone you don't. From session five, with the spirit of Cynthia's father:

> He says, "*I was not prepared to meet a religious figure...*" So whoever this person was that came in, was not a religious icon. Did he have a brother that passed?"

Cynthia said that he had. Her father kept filling me in on some details:

> This was a younger male figure…One that comes forward. The brother that passed, there was trauma around his death.

Again, another affirmative from Cynthia that her father's brother was younger, with significant trauma surrounding his passing:

> He's making me feel like, his brother's death was much more serious.

Though I did not allow Cynthia to elaborate on just *how much more serious* the brother's passing was, she did confirm that it was much worse than her father's. I continued:

> And it startled him to see his brother walk forward and say, *"This is where you're at."* A lot of stuff surrounding his brother's death…The brother had to coax him to go into the tunnel. He shows his brother almost kind of grab him by the arm and pull him…The brother would not let him stay. I think he appealed at that point to your dad's emotional side *"…If you stay it's going to be much harder."*

And from session seven, with Debbie's father:

> Relative…His brother. Did one of his brothers go before him?

Debbie confirmed that, like Cynthia, her father had a brother who had passed earlier in life. Her father continued filling me with images and feelings:

> He places the individual to his side. He shows him…One that he would consider weird and screwy? He draws this weird shape and never in a straight line. For his parents, dad went first, correct? He says dad came first, then mother.

Debbie confirmed that all of this was accurate—his brother *was* considered the oddball in the family, and that his father had passed first and then his mother.

For my sitter M.G., her deceased mother had been the follower of a Hindu guru, indicating him by first initial earlier in the sitting and then referencing him in response to this question:

> There's reference to family members—her parents and the other one who came up earlier...Did the guru pass before she did? She shows me Gandhi.

Indeed, the guru had died earlier and was using the image of Gandhi to show his passing.

In one interview, the deceased described the reunion with her family like this:

> She makes me feel like there weren't any religious figures there. The family alone was enough to get her excited. She's making me feel like *"Oh my gosh, all this beloved energy from the family."*

From session thirteen, as divulged by the spirit of Gabi's mother:

> She saw her mom and dad...and reference to a third person who is a male. I don't know if mom lost a child...but it's definitely someone in the family. Not a grandfather...But she says, "At *this stage of the game it was just my relatives because they knew I would feel most comfortable with them."* They were escorting her on the journey.

In a few cases, spirit guides did accompany the returning family members. These spiritual helpers were usually seen as strangers, but were recognized as having deep spiritual connections in comparison to the others. From session eleven, with the spirit of Terri's grandmother, Rose, who had been married numerous times in her life:

> She says, *"I have my husbands—and my brother is here, too."* Then she is going, *"Ooh,"* about seeing these "other" people. She's like, *"I'm not going to put religion in the framework,"* but

she's saying, *"These are the higher-up people."* She acknowledges them being there, but not with religious connotation.

For Brandon (who had committed suicide), he was immediately met by a benevolent team from the light. This is how he explained it to me:

He would call it a guide—and this is terminology he got from other people. He did not meet a religious figure…I think there was a relative on the outskirts, but they did not come forward. He says, *"I was met…"* He shows me two or three entities that come forward.

He says, *"You don't know what it's like when you go through this…You do not understand the magnitude of how it feels."* He's definitely wanting to make the point that if you think you feel alive right now where you are at, when you go through this kind of event and that light encompasses you and you see those people…It is a much greater feeling than what you normally experience when you are alive.

At that point, a heavy weight came over him. He says, *"It's from me, it's from me, it's not from them."* It was at that point when he entered the light and saw the people that he suddenly realized, *"Oh my God, I think I did something I shouldn't have done."*

He says, *"I did not argue with them…I wanted them to…"* In a way he was kind of being defensive…I think as soon as he saw them, he was afraid they were going to start judging him or reprimanding him…He just was telling them, *"You don't know the people I was having to deal with…You don't know the people I was having to deal with."* To me, he's making me feel like he felt that his condition and his situation were more the result of other people rather than his own inability to make decisions.

Only on one or two occasions did someone make me feel they had met some kind of religious figure. There may be a few reasons for this. As mentioned earlier, the transition may be better facilitated by people the newly deceased personally recognize. The other reason for the rarity of seeing religious figures may be that the deceased wasn't a very religious person to begin with (though a few did claim to be). As we'll see in Volume II, religious figures come with an interesting background. For the most part, it appears the transition of dying is not something done alone. Friends and family are there to greet you and herald the good times ahead.

4

Was There a Life Review?
How Would You Describe It?

The Life Review is another one of the recurrent themes reported in Near Death Experience accounts. I always found it intriguing that someone who wasn't slated to officially "die" received such a review, yet thought it quite logical that when life was truly over such a review would be not only possible, but incredibly practical and enlightening.

After reviewing the fourteen responses to this question, it became clear that those on the Other Side have a level of compassion and understanding that is equal to (if not beyond) sainthood. As you'll see, they really take care in managing the mind and emotions of the newcomer into the realm of spirit. Depending on one's level of fear, trauma, thought processes, and probably other personal traits, the Life Review process takes on an individualistic nature, though there are definite similarities throughout. It appears the Other Side can tailor each new arrival's review for maximum benefit and minimal trauma.

In nearly all cases, the person receiving the Life Review was accompanied either by relatives or spiritual guides—however, these guests kept their distance, as if to allow a sense of privacy for the individual. Only in a few cases did accompanying family members or spiritual guides enter into the newcomer's "personal space," and when they did, it was to provide comfort for what the deceased was thinking and feeling. In all cases, my sitters' deceased family and friends reported that there was no sense of judgment coming from any of the people there with them, only love and compassion. And this played out in how the Life Review was revealed. Let's start with Brandon, from session two:

> He says that was one of the best things they did for him…He says, "*What they did in my Life Review…they made it small in terms of size, and made me larger than what I was viewing, so I could take all of it in, and yet not overwhelm me. It was the most loving and caring thing I had seen and ever had done. Even though the problems were still there and being shown to me…they created the imagery in such a way…They kept saying you're bigger than this, you're bigger than this. Can you see that, that you're bigger than this?*" He's saying, "*They didn't dismiss the conditions, they didn't dismiss the problems, but they wanted to keep me…*" He didn't have a lot of control over his emotions because the whole point of keeping him larger was because they understood he could get emotionally caught up in what he was viewing, and it would just make him spiral down into more despair, and they didn't want that to happen, they wanted to keep him above that; it would be harder to heal.

It was obvious from the imagery and description how much love and compassion were being showered upon him.

The most common feature the Life Review took was showing the course of a life from the point-of-view of either seeing it on a screen or being immersed in it like a holographic recording. Again, this is probably determined based upon how much an arriving soul can handle when reviewing the life he or she just left. An added bonus to me in this question was how some spirits were able to relate the course of their lives back to me, giving small glimpses into their histories, such as the following:

> She starts the process like a film reel starting—click, click, click.
> Was she born around the 4th of July or a flag holiday?

At this point, my sitter said, "no," but it became clear a moment later why there was so much fanfare.

When she starts the film reel, I hear the parade marching music, like a celebration. Here you are, you're thrust into the world and it's a real celebration…I don't know why I'm seeing a flag.

At that moment, my sitter, Marti, revealed that her mother was the first of her generation to be born in Czechoslovakia—and that her birth was a magnificent celebration for the entire family. I continued with what was coming through:

She's telling me there were a good two or three times in her life when she made some bad mistakes, and so when these times came up in the Life Review, there's this dread that comes over her. She says, "*It comes and it goes and it passes, and you're all right. You don't get criticized for them.*"

Marti rightfully asked "Can she share what some of the mistakes are?" Immediately, her mother started shooting me with imagery which produced a rather vivid picture:

Do you know if she was going to get married to another guy and didn't go through with it?

Indeed, such a circumstance had been a troubling time in her mother's life—another boyfriend had asked her to marry him, yet she declined. I revealed to Marti how I was receiving the information:

One of the points has to do with the male…It's a coming together and going apart with this marriage feel to it. I don't know how bad that is in the culture, but it's one those things that she puts this in a field of darkness. It's like, "*This was a bad point in my life…*"

From session twelve, with my sitter Kourtnie's deceased father, as it was given to me:

For him, they played his life out in front of him like it was on a movie screen. He laughs and says, *"I got to see all the crap I did as a kid."* He takes me back to the past, and says, *"I was a hellion."*

Of course, Kourtnie confirmed that her father had a reputation in his youth for creating a ton of trouble. The session continued:

But he grew out of it, is what he's showing me …As a kid he was a real hellion, but when he got older, he started to mature, got new ideas, started to realize things were different…Created a whole new personality for himself, going from childhood to adult.

Kourtnie again confirmed that personality maturation was indeed how the course of his life progressed. I went on:

When he saw the changes in his life through the Life Review, how he grew out of that, he really had a special pride in himself that he never gave himself when he was alive. He saw that he wasn't a one-dimensional person. He did change, he did shift. He really grew into something way back here (in his youth) he never would have considered possible.

From session five, with the spirit of Cynthia's father, I was prompted to question, "Did he have eye problems really bad toward the end?" Cynthia confirmed that, yes, her father had severe eye problems. I continued:

He says the first thing that happened when he got out of the tunnel, his eyesight was perfect, to the point that everything was almost too bright for him to look at.
He makes me feel like, *"As soon as I got out of the tunnel, the Life Review thing started."* I mean, there was no sit down and get ready for it. It was all of a sudden boom…*"Because memories are fresh,"* he says…What he's showing me…he's either sitting or standing…and the Life Review is playing out in front of him, but it's only this big (like a small box) and hovering

right out in front of me like watching it on a video screen. He shows…Did he have a sister?

Yes, turns out he did. And Cynthia was able to validate the other information her father was giving me as I continued:

And he says their relationship was close. He's showing me the stuff he really enjoyed was reviewing the relationship to his sister when they were younger.

And from session thirteen, with Gabi's mother, her memorable past events were brought up during the Life Review:

She says the Life Review started out right in front of her, like a projection. Did her family move when she was like eight or nine? There's this reference to something traumatic happening, and that's the only way I can describe it…Something pulled and taken away, something lost…Being physically moved.

Gabi couldn't place the reference to moving at the time of the session. But after talking with her mother's best friend from childhood, she confirmed that indeed, her family had moved from Pennsylvania to Baltimore—and her mother absolutely hated it.

In one case, the spirit of Sarah's Muslim grandfather was very concerned about judgment. He reported how it took a little time before the review could get underway:

He draws a space here and says the Life Review didn't happen right away…"I needed to get calmed down…" He's making me feel like they let him kind of sit there for a few minutes, to get his bearings, or come to the reality that life is over, you're still alive, it's okay…You're safe. It's that feeling of needing to feel safe. "I've got to feel safe." So he needed to get that in order first.

Then he says, "Drop down, they dropped me down into the Life Review…The reason they dropped me down was to make me feel more grounded…" There's some conflict between having wealth and spirituality. I don't know in the religion if being wealthy has a negative connotation attached to it, but there's this disconnect that I think he was worried about how he handled his money, having that much money might not bode well for him; that he may be judged negatively for it. I think he was worried about that—something to do with money. They drop him down for the Life Review, just to give a sense of grounding. Whether or not they physically dropped him down, I don't know…"I just got to be dropped down."

Interestingly, he was considered a wealthy man while alive, as he owned multiple properties. Then once the review started, it took on different forms for different people, as Sarah's grandfather continued:

Then he says, "They showed it to me as large as life." It's kind of like, you're sitting down on the floor and you're watching your life around you in true size, true form.

In a completely different fashion, Grace's grandmother from my fourth session described it as more of an internal viewing inside the mind:

She says, "They laid me down on the ground, and then they had me look up at the sky. In the sky, there was peace. Inside my head, they started showing me visions about my life. And they were allowing me to tell them what it was I was feeling about the things I was seeing." Was there a really negative event that happened in her early childhood? She's making me feel like…I want to go way back…They allowed her to go back to herself as a little girl to see this darkness…They kept her supported and allowed her to go back and go through that experience. And she says, "When they do this, when this happens, there are points that come up…points that come up…and these points are realities of your life and those things you don't like…" She says, "They do not judge you per these points you do not like." In fact, she says they were actually quite silent…"They just want you to *sit with it; they want you to be with who you were and what your life was. Then they sat me up, and there was this knowingness and lovingness in their eyes that said it's all right; everything is going to be all right."*

One of the other features that became common throughout the Life Review process was that the deceased were able to feel how their thoughts and actions affected other people while alive on earth. In many cases, the deceased reported feeling how they made other people feel during their existence, as was related from this part of the transcript:

He says, *"I'm hooked into everybody...I'm hooked into everybody."* This is the *"I'm feeling what other people are feeling."* As he's reviewing his life, he can see and feel how everybody reacted to him, and being hooked in. He's showing me lines going from him to everybody that he's dealing with as he's going through the Life Review. He says he had a really positive childhood; that he liked reviewing those points. And he places his parents way up here on a pedestal.

From session seven, the spirit of Debbie's father also talked about his role in peoples lives and the resultant emotions:

He's making me feel like it's much more vivid than just a memory. You can feel all the emotions...It's like showing me a running film clip. He says, *"Watch the film clip, you can see all this stuff being plastered on everybody in your imaginings, as if to say, you're seeing a much greater aspect of those people at the time than what you had when you were alive. You know what they're feeling,"* he says.

From session nine, the spirit-brother of my sitter reported on realizing the truth about himself and how his personality influenced his life:

Did he change personality throughout his life, like becoming another person and another?

My sitter, Teri K. (different from Terri of my eleventh sitting) confirmed that, yes, her brother had shifted personalities rather distinctly several times during the course of his earthly journey. Her brother continued:

> When it comes to the Life Review, he shows me four different beings, as if to say, "*I was four different people and each one of these I was able to see and able to experience. I saw myself for who and what I was.*" He's making me feel like, in that moment in the Life Review, you can no longer lie to yourself.

And finding the truth was definitely the impetus for Diane in my fourteenth sitting. While alive, she appeared to be someone who took things lightly and with ease—always joking and being rather flippant. However, that changed when she had a chance to really review her past:

> When she was here, she didn't take herself too seriously. She's making me feel like, "*I took everything very lightly to everyone outside, but this was a façade.*" When she got into the Life Review…She grabs my heart and says, "*I paid attention. In life, I wouldn't have had that appearance, but in the Life Review…I was very in sync with what was being shown.*" She took things personally.

The spirit of Marti's mother in session ten summed up the Life Review process nicely, I thought:

> She shows me that once you get through the whole process of this Life Review, she shows it to me as water under the bridge… She says you get a whole new perspective on everything you did in your life. The imagery she's showing me is that we live in a two-dimensional world, and when you pass, you get to see it in three dimensions, and you go, "*Whoa! This is what it's really about…Or this is how things really happened and what they are…And this changes my view on everything.*" At that point, you go, "*Okay, the experiences were real, they were there, now I've got this whole different view of them…I can finally let go of*

some of this stuff." The whole different perspective allows an inner healing process to occur.

In one case, my sitter's mother had spent a good deal of her life in reflection, introspection, and attempting to live in spiritual harmony with the universe. When it came to this question, her unique response was "I didn't need it." Because of her awareness of her own thoughts and actions while alive, at the time of her passing she had sufficient wisdom to bypass the point of the Life Review!

It is apparent the Life Review is there to reveal how we as individuals interacted within a holistic environment. We have often heard that there is no separation between ourselves and our neighbors—that we are essentially One. The Life Review illustrates this notion with amazing clarity, but not so overwhelming that it crushes a person's spirit. From session eleven, with Terri's grandmother, Rose:

> She wants to take your hand and say, *"You would not believe it."* She says you would not believe, they report everything. *"I saw everything. I saw the things I didn't want anybody else to see."* And she was very guarded when certain events started playing out in front of her that she thought were private. And when these started coming up, it was like, *"Oh my God, don't watch. You shouldn't even be aware of this."* Even during these times where it was incredibly private, they (two ex-husbands) were still in her sphere as a support mechanism. And of course, the guides are there, but she could tell, she could feel and knew, they weren't judging her for what she had done and what she was seeing in the Life Review. And she was glad to have the two people there.
>
> It's one of those things where, it's going on right at the moment, and you just have to go through it. If it were a perfect world, she obviously wouldn't have the two people there with her. But since it was going on at the moment, she just went through it. And she's saying, *"The good parts of the Life Review and the parts that were the fun times and the celebratory times, made up for those bad points in our history"* that she wanted

to keep in. She's referencing Disneyland as to what the high points felt like. [Incidentally, most of the family trips she had taken were to Disneyland.]

The confusion of how her life was played out before her permeated the question. When it came to those areas where she was exclaiming, "Oh my God, you shouldn't be seeing this!", she gave me a whopping sense of "and how did they record this?" It was a question that fascinated the spirit of Diane, as she came from a scientific background while on earth. This is how it came out in the transcript:

> The Life Review was also a scientific curiosity for her. She was wondering how this was happening, how her life was being shown back to her. She was hooked up emotionally to it, while at the same time she was thinking from the left-brain, asking, "How is this happening? What's the mechanism for this? How is this being shown to me? How are they reproducing this for me? How did they grab this information?"

And finally, from the spirit of Gabi's mother in session thirteen, as she played out the images within my consciousness:

> The Life Review is shown to her like a holographic play that is being played out in front of her. Everything is life-size. It's a projection...They've taken some of the intensity out of it. She says, "As I'm feeling this, I know it is meant to inform me what I was thinking and doing...'Cause when you are in that moment of thinking and doing, you are not always aware of your motivations." But that was what the Life Review was revealing... And towards the last twenty to thirty years of her life, she had gotten really bitter.

Gabi burst out with a resounding "Yes." For decades, her mother had become incredibly disenchanted with life. I continued:

> She shows me going down the timeline—the bitterness, the

feeling of depression. She says, in this course of the Life Review, as she's going through the decades with this remorse, her mother (Gabi's grandmother) comes up and holds her hand. It's like, *"You're going to be fine; you're going to be okay."* She says the heavenly hosts did not judge. They did make her feel protected. There was this sense of *"They're not going to judge me, they're not going to hurt me; they are supporting me."* There was nothing verbal, it was just a feeling.

For the most part, the Life Review is something about 99% of us will experience after we pass into spirit. It is designed to reveal who we were and why we did certain things while alive on earth, and how those actions or inactions affected the greater whole of our environment and fellow spiritual humans. It is not meant to be a show for someone to judge us, condemn us, or even congratulate us, but to grant us a wider understanding of our impulses, motivations, and fears. The Life Review clues us in to what we still need to work on in order to better enjoy and celebrate life as we move ahead into the world of spirit and other incarnations. A universal axiom is that all things are connected and One. The Life Review reveals this unity and how each of us affects the web of life we encounter.

5

Was There a Transition Place or Holding Ground Before Going to a Place You Would Now Call "Home"? If So, What Took Place There?

I have heard from other sources that once a Life Review was over, a debriefing of what came out of the review was discussed with family members, guides, et al. I took it on faith that such an event occurred and didn't bother to ask about that debriefing as part of the questions (although during the sittings many spirits referenced their debriefings anyway). Instead, I was more intrigued by the notion that the newly departed spirit was then sent to a "holding ground" before being "shipped off" to their next destination. This holding ground has often been referred to as a kind of subway station or airport terminal, where passengers are whisked off in several directions to different parts of the spiritual world.

It seems that everyone starts out in roughly the same place—a tunnel or mist, followed by a neutral location for a Life Review. But then it stands to reason that not everyone moves on to the exact same location afterward. That is, we may all arrive at the same "airport" and get checked in, but that doesn't mean we're necessarily boarding the same flight and going to the same destination!

Sometimes the transition to the holding ground after a Life Review isn't so simple as going from A to B. Many of my sitters' relatives reported still being somewhat shocked by the details and revelations of the Life Review, as spoken by Rose, Terri's grandmother:

She was really stunned from the Life Review. She's showing me that, *"I didn't want to move forward right away."* She kind of walks over to the side, sits down, and was just flabbergasted. And she's making me feel like, *"They just let me do that. They just let me...It was like shock. It was like traumatic shock. To be able to see the details of your life flashed back in front of you in that way..."* She's saying, *"It encompassed everything. Not only what I did, but what everybody felt. Everybody I had affected. When it was done, I couldn't just say, 'Okay, it's done, it's all over'"...It* was a shell shock to her consciousness. They allowed her to sit there for a while and just absorb that.

She must have had some really traumatic experiences. She started to cry. It was a pity cry. That's when the spirit guides stepped forward and said, *"You don't need to do this. We're not going to go there."* That's when she had her main guide, a higher guide, and a lower guide, pull her off the ground and tell her, *"Okay, you're all right. You're going to be fine."* And when they reached down and grabbed her, they infused that forgiveness and that love into her consciousness. At that point, she was ready to move on.

She understood that those events in the Life Review were going to be retained in her consciousness, in the record of herself, so to speak. But it was not to define who she was. That's what they were trying to tell her. *"Yes, these events happened. Yes, they are part of who you are. But they don't define you— because you are still going to move forward and change."*

Moreover, some spirits chose to deliberate and debrief, as was the case with my first and seventh sitters:

Before moving on, there was a debriefing. Again, it wasn't a judgment call or chastising, it was more like, *"See how you could have done this differently?"* He's talking about attachment, about how before he was allowed to move, there were feelings of attachment he had relating to certain events he had to let go of...

He says for the Life Review, he had several people there—beings there—that when the review was done, they were very impressed with him...He communicated through his Life Review with these people. He wasn't one to sit there and just take it. He really stepped away from the absorption of it and was critiquing everything and communicating about it with the guides there...really talking it over with them. They were really impressed with his openness and willing to discuss the events.

For Diane, her debriefing was facilitated by her deceased father:

Dad took over the debriefing. He had better ideas of how the mind works, how the psychological mind works...He said, "*I know you've buried this stuff your whole life.*"...He really brought comfort and...fleshed the breadth of the relationship out.

For those newcomers who had an especially trying life on earth or deleterious reaction to the Life Review, there was a separate space set aside for the soul to be cleansed and spiritually recharged before moving on. Diane, in particular, was one of them. As you'll see, she started to reveal the contents of what she had buried since the time of her childhood:

She shows me bypassing the holding ground...And they take her to another spot...Did she lose a friend or a younger person in her youth that she felt responsible for? Did she feel responsible for her brother's death? She's saying, "*They had to get that out of me.*" She's showing me that "*I felt responsible for passing somebody.*"

Indeed, it was exactly as she had shown it to me. When she was a child, she had briefly left her little brother with his bicycle outside on the street while she went back inside to fetch something. During her momentary absence, a car come along and accidentally hit her brother, killing him instantly. It was something she never forgave herself for her entire life. It was something she needed to deal with before moving on. The session continued:

They sat her down with her brother and really worked on that...because she had to let go of all that emotion, and it was like this big bursting. There was all this shame and guilt..."*I feel responsible for this person that passed.*" Those two had to come together to understand the dynamics and for her to release that. They wouldn't let her go to the holding ground until she had done that.

From session nine, with the deceased brother of Teri K.:

He's saying, *"Before I went to the holding ground, they pulled me aside."*

At this point, I picked up my white board and drew a sort of map that I was seeing in my head, displaying sections where the deceased was being led:

Here's the Life Review area...He's saying, *"Typically when they're done, they go to this holding area. For me, they dropped me over here. Part of it was...energy revitalization...They weren't healing me, but they were amping me up."* So he must have left with a low amount of energy. And he's making me feel like it's only a part of it...He's saying that, *"Up here there's counseling going on...Different points of view are given me...Then I got this 'energy up' and then went over here to the holding ground."*

From session twelve, with the spirit of Kourtnie's father:

Prior to getting to the holding ground, he did meet his biological father and a couple of other people. Mother was there. His grandfather who raised him was there. He says, *"Before I hit this other place, there was this family reunion that happened."* And then he shows me...getting the power up. As you mentioned, he had depression really bad. It really wore him down energy-wise and made him sluggish. He was almost a prisoner in himself. So here's this moment where he's getting ready to move on, he shows it to me as them pulling this sluggish energy out of him and cleaning him out; making him bright again. And he says it was easy to do after seeing the Life Review, *"Because I had that realization that 'hey, things weren't that bad, after I grew out of that phase.'"*

And for Brandon, our suicide:

He's saying in his case...He had to get counseling first...He's saying, *"They pulled me away, took me to a place..."* and they "fed" him. They did something with his energy to nourish it. It's like, *"I was hungry; they fed me."* But this has to do with inner things, it has nothing to do with food; it's all inner stuff. Did his family have a dog?

All of a sudden, Brandon's spirit had showed me the image of a dog. To me, such a thing is quite unusual, as I don't normally receive pets. The more I focused in, the more I saw the dog looking up at the ceiling. I continued:

I think the dog saw him after he passed. I'm sure of it. I'm sure that's what he's referencing. As he's in this space getting the power up...he shows me this.

I began to draw an image of Brandon in the space on the Other Side, then connected a line to a drawing of a house:

This is the space he's at and he draws this line as if to say, *"Back at home, this is home."* He goes down to the ground and shows me a dog, and the dog is looking up and he sees him. He wanted to somehow...It wasn't that he even wanted, I think it happened randomly, I don't even think he knew what he was doing, he just started thinking of the people he had left behind. And he somehow got a glimpse and the dog caught it.

When it came to the actual location of this holding ground, it appeared that it could take on many forms. For some, they described it like an airport hub; for others, more like a beautiful country meadow or field. And they also mentioned they were not alone—others who had recently passed were also in this space. Comments came through about how in the conglomeration of people was a mixture of excitement, awe, and quiet reflection. In all cases, the subjects knew intuitively that they were destined for some location beyond the hub, though they did not know exactly where that place was or what it looked like. Nevertheless, they were able to feel some kind of pull in their energy which told them a grand future awaited. From session twelve, with Kourtnie's father:

> "*Now, I go into the field,*" he says. He describes it similar to a football field. He says this is where he stood with many others who had just made it here. He's saying, "*Remember how we got jostled around in the big crowd?*" He's putting me in a concert-type crowd where you're packed in with a lot of people... "*Remember how we got really hot, hard to breathe, that sort of thing?*" He says it wasn't like that. There were a lot of people, but it wasn't really that bad.
>
> What took place there? He gives me this weird funky energy. It was just this place where, because everybody has just come there, he's assuming they are just coming from their Life Review...He says there is all this emotion going on. Some are blissed out, some are freaked out, some are very quiet...He says it's this whole range of stuff. He says he himself was calm, and said, "*Well, I've made it this far, I'm still alive, so goddamn— I'm going forward somewhere.*" Part of the reason he's bringing all this up, too, is because he didn't like drama.

This mention of not liking drama was a key character description for Kourtnie's dad. When I mentioned it, her face lit up and she exclaimed "That's totally him." I continued:

> He's looking at people and asking, "*What's the drama?*" But he knows he's going to be fine, but he doesn't know what's going

to happen next. He just knows something is going to happen.

The busy hub image continued with the spirit of Michael, Leah's friend:

> He says there are many people. It's not that you're alone—
> There are other people also swooping into this place. He uses
> the *"ocean waves breaking"* reference, of people dying in large
> numbers every day—waves hitting, crashing the shore, and
> pulling back. There are so many people coming and going all
> the time, you're going to be crammed into these places. He
> says, *"Once you're in the hub, there is a feeling or essence that is
> attached to you in some way, so when it comes to the home place
> out of the hub, it's already programmed into your consciousness;
> it really requires no thinking—it's a vibration, it's a feeling, it's
> something that creates a bond to a location, if you want to call it
> a location."* He says, *"It takes you to that next level."*

Sarah's Muslim grandfather from session six described the crowded transition place like this:

> He says there is a holding ground and he's making me feel like
> this is not a place people really know about or talk about. It's
> not simply "boom" you're here and then "boom" you're there.
> He draws a circle, as if to say there was this hub…The transition
> point, the transition place…He says it was *"a place where many
> of us who just made the transition were brought together"*…He
> shows me as an analogy, taking a bunch of farm animals and
> herding them into a pen…It's just there to herd them together
> and get them localized into a central place.
>
> Some people were very ecstatic, excited, happy…He was
> not as joyous as some of the others. And he's showing me
> there were different nationalities, different identities alongside
> of him. There was no one ethnicity or one religion accounted
> for; it was a mixture of all the varieties of humankind.
>
> It was at this area, that there was this sense within him that
> something greater was going on…There was a definite feeling

attached to it, like, *"Okay, when we hit this area, we just knew inside ourselves that something great was on the horizon. We really couldn't pinpoint what it was, we just knew it was there."* At that point, there's this huge sigh of relief. There's almost a recognition to the feeling, even though you don't quite know what it is. You recognize it, you trust it, you relax with it. I feel he started to relax. But he wasn't joyful. He shows me some people were absolutely giddy. That wasn't him. I don't know if he was the kind to be more level while he was here and not real emotional, but seeing these people over here, it's kind of like, *"Okay, that's a little much."*

The spirit of Debbie's father agreed with having a knowingness of one's direction:

He's showing me they (spirit guides) shoved him off, and there was a holding ground, but he's making me feel like, *"My time there was so small,"* it's almost like, *"I could have just bypassed this."* It's like, *"I already had some kind of knowledge or inclination of what's waiting for me...I knew what was waiting for me."* He was there and then he was off.

For Grace's grandmother who lived in Hong Kong, she described the transition place to me in the form of a multi-level temple:

She's making me feel like, *"When I got done here with the Life Review thing, the holding ground was up a level, like in a temple."* So they took her up into this temple-setting, higher level, and she's with multiple people and with lots of people...She says, *"These are other people who have died around the same time I did, and who have just completed their Life Reviews. There is this place we're being situated before moving on to the next place."* She's saying, *"We don't know where we're going out of here, just that we will be going somewhere. There's this recognition inside of us that's telling us we're going someplace. We're okay."* She says you're standing there with this bunch of people...

Some people are in a state of shock, due to the Life Review. Some people are actually socializing about what they experienced.

"What we all noticed was a 'compelling' inside of us that was going to lift us somewhere into wherever this new place was where we were at. We didn't know where, but we knew that we could trust it; there was a feeling to it." She says, *"I was a little bit humbled..."* humbled is the feeling...She's making me feel like she talked to a few people there, but it wasn't like socializing... it wasn't a whole lot of talking, because she was still caught in the emotion of what she had just gone through.

When it finally came time to move on, I was fortunate to receive a few very interesting visuals from the deceased. From session ten, with the spirit of Marti's mother as she described her departure from the hub:

She's seeing swirling bits of energy...The people get enveloped and disappear, as if they rise up and disappear. She says after a few seconds, *"I look back down at the field and saw it disappear. And then I was surrounded by space. And then..."* Then she says there was this fog...*"And when the fog cleared I was in a whole different environment."* She was not in a very industrialized neighborhood when she grew up, correct? [This was correct.]

She makes me feel like, *"I'm dropping down in the middle of the street and there's...this is how things used to be when I was a kid...there's not a whole lot of industry..."* not even sure if there was electricity...it just feels very old to me.

The spirit of Gabi's mother (who didn't like speed, if you'll recall) described her departure similarly:

She was told *"shut your eyes for this."* She could feel...*"It's an odd feeling,"* she says, *"because I can feel the ground beneath my feet, but I can feel myself moving."* Weird motion sense... She knows she is moving up and around. She says, she did open her eyes one time to see what was happening and all she could see were streaks of light passing by her. She's saying she felt insulated, like I'm not flying out in deep space. She's saying, *"I felt secure, but there was this streaking of light. Then all of a sudden it just stopped, and I opened my eyes and I was outside again; but I was in a completely different space and location. And then there was more than just mom and dad; there was a whole group of people there,"* and they were cheering her on like it was a party.

So it appears that once a Life Review is finished, the new arrivals from earth are rounded up in some fashion, with an intuitive sense of where they are heading next. No clue was given to me as to *how* the groups are chosen, but it appears ethnicity and religion play no part in the overall structure of a group. Perhaps there is no defined structure beyond grouping by recentness of death, as people die at all times, day or night, and under any type of condition. Once it is realized that death is not the end and that each person goes on, the type of death does not matter as a possible criteria defining the groups. Quite frankly, nobody in *The Afterlife Interviews* made me feel like the groups are "filtered" by any one type of criteria, thus a time-based group would consist of all kinds of people.

At any rate, not everyone is destined for the same location, and this may very well be by choice, preference, or other factors (which we will get into later). So once the Life Review has past, there is still this in-between location where the Soul checks in before disembarking into felicity.

Any Other Comments About the Death Experience?

I have ended this section on the dying process with this open-ended question. The way I figured it, up to this point the questions asked were guiding the discussion; there was always the possibility I might have missed something. Besides, I wanted the deceased to have an opportunity to inject their own opinions. It is so reassuring to hear and feel what they chose to say.

From session one, with the spirit of Michael:

> *"It's actually incredibly easy and painless. The pain part is like, two seconds before it happens because of 'what's going to happen next?' The pain and fear part is all on the earthly side of the realms. The actual movement, the actual walking from one doorway into the other is totally painless. It's actually very freeing,"* he says, as if he was trapped (don't know if he felt trapped in the body or bodily conditions). There was this feeling of freedom coming through for him.

From session two, with Brandon:

> *"Don't do it the way I did it, if you have to go through it."* When he says, *"Don't do it the way I did it,"* he's not coming from doing

the "*Live your life grand and die naturally*"—that sort of thing. He's coming very much from his own experience in saying, "*Just don't do it the way I did it. Choose something else.*"

From session three, with Nancy's father:

"*It's peaceful and you will have friends that will help you.*" He's making me feel like, he kind of considered himself a bit of a coward when it came to the dying process; not a tough guy. It's one of those comments of "*If I can get through it, anybody can get through it. I would've been the biggest wussie if it were tough,*" that sort of sensation. The sense is, "*If it were going to be tough, I wouldn't have done it.*" "*Pleasant*" is not his word, it's "*easy.*" Easy, in terms of the process, not how it feels.

From session five, with Cynthia's father on the Other Side:

He says, "*It's one of the most freeing points of your existence.*" He writes the word "*defines*"…"*It defines a big global aspect of your being here…It's like putting a puzzle piece into the puzzle and finally getting an idea of what the picture is supposed to look like.*" It gave him perspective on why he came here…He was at a little bit higher elevation of consciousness…He had some pretty deep ideas about the nature of the universe. He says he had some of this knowledge here, "*So when I saw this stuff, I was able to put the puzzle pieces together.*" He understood where the puzzle pieces went as a result of going through this process."

From session six, with Sarah's Muslim grandfather:

He flashes the word "*pageantry*" in front of me…He says, "*It's the pageantry of the life you left behind. The death experience is your chronicle being played to you. It is the hosting of your life. To rejoice in it, to re-encounter things in it that you may have forgotten or you may have lost…*" Product, product…"*It's a product of your life...It reveals the product of your life."* And when he says that, he makes me feel like, it's something to be very joyful for. Now that he's been away for so long, he now feels like the giddy person, when it comes to the death process. He wasn't that way while he was going through it, but in retrospect, that's really what it's all about. It is the pageantry of your life, to honor it and feel joy for what you've contributed and what you've done. He says, *"Praise be to...praise be..."* It's about praising life rather than coming at it from the perspective of being judgmental and pointing a finger at yourself.

From session ten, with the spirit of Marti's mother:

I'm getting that paradise is a whole lot freer than what we think it is. She takes the garden of Eden paradise and starts taking all of this white light energy and ascends it up into the sky like butterflies. It's like, it's so much freer and open than what we've known. I feel really, *really* free—there's no confinement, there's no chains. *"Alternatives and possibilities exist,"* she says. As she shows me the butterflies and energy flowing around, there's no confinement. Any predefined things that have to happen are really just possibilities, and they're not written in stone.

From session fourteen, with the spirit of Diane:

She says, *"Don't be afraid of it. You can walk through it with confidence."* She's backing that up with—most people have this big fear, when they finally die...They have this fear of losing control...But she makes me feel like, *"You can remain in your power, in your level of confidence. Nobody is wanting to take that from you...Everyone has this big judgment fear..."* She's like, *"Just forget that...Stay grounded in your being and you will walk out okay."*

And finally, I'd like to end with session nine. Teri K.'s brother was coming through and he said it so succinctly, and the imagery was so poignant:

> He comes up to the chest and says, *"It's so wonderful to take a full breath. And this is really living."*

7

Were There Aspects of Your Identity That You Lost When You Died? Were There Things You Gained? What?

I was curious that when people die, do they lose more than just their physical bodies? Because we are so well integrated into the three dimensional physical world, I wondered how being disentangled from the environment after death might affect someone. Likewise, since being divorced from physical reality and wedded to the world of spirit, does a newly deceased arrival gain something unknown, which he or she lacked prior to dying?

The results from the question seemed to point to a change more in one's mind—of how one thinks—rather than anything tangible. People often believe that when one sheds the mortal coil, all knowledge about the universe will become available to them. Apparently that is not the case, though we are certainly not left feeling inadequate in the face of our ignorance. But in terms of personality and all those qualities that make up one's inner perception of self, all of that remains when we pass over.

Nancy's father in session three begins by describing the continuity of one's self-identity:

> He says for his identity, he didn't lose anything. In fact, he tried holding onto it, because he was..."*I'm in unfamiliar territory here.*" It's almost like culture shock…You go into a new country…So he actually clung to his own sense of identity.

In terms of gaining, he makes me feel like he gained a better sense of how to loosen up. And the way he shows that to me is…He comes in holding onto his identity…*"I'm tight, holding onto it, and then it loosens up."* It's all soft and transparent and "whoosh."

In terms of like any major knowledge that gives you magical powers, no. But he says you do gain a different perspective on yourself. *"It's all very much centered around you,"* he says… *"Your development through this process."*

From session five, Cynthia's father adds to the message:

Aspects to identity…He's making me feel like, *"I will always be who I am…The personality doesn't change…"* So the memories you have of the way he was, the way he did things, the way he reacted, the way he responded…that still is the way he is. He carries that forward. It's almost like…*"mold"* is not the right word…*"template"*…He says there is a template to the personality and it's this that carries forward. Gain…gain… he says, *"Yes, you gain a new perspective and new awareness."* Then he says, *"That's only because you're in a new location now."* Example: When you look at your own house through the window of your neighbor. You've got your perspective while on earth, then you pass, and then you just look at things at a different angle. This is the gain that you get—this new angle. The whole notion of total immense knowledge about the nature of the universe being granted, he says, *"no."*

Additionally, Sarah's Muslim grandfather confirms the same:

He's making me feel like it was a relief that he got to retain his identity. I think he feared that when you die, you would lose a part of yourself…that you would be absorbed into something greater and be no more. He's making me feel like, *"I'm really relieved I got to keep my identity."* And he shows me taking a blanket off, as if to say, "*I was able to get rid of a whole bunch of other stuff that never needed to be there in the first place.*" He says, "*I took the cloak off that was covering my eyes.*" He's making me feel like, in wearing the cloak…I'm hearing, "*Shut down world.*" As if to say, the only thing that mattered was what was in the boundaries of the cloak. Everything else was bad, wrong, evil—whatever you want to classify it—when it really wasn't. The cloak was a bogus perception.

This notion of bogus perceptions was also expressed in session fourteen with Diane. Remember earlier how I mentioned she had a scientific background? It came out in her answer to this question, as evidenced from the transcript:

She keeps showing me her brain and pulling it out. She had preconceived notions of how the nature of the world or the universe worked and that's what got pulled out of her. She shows the word "*physics*" and pulls that out…and says that went bye-bye. What did she gain? She says, "*When I lost that part, it didn't matter.*" You know, if some people had to divorce themselves from such ideas, it could be crushing to the ego and spirit; she's like, "*I still got to retain my personality and way of being…*" She says, "*Losing that, I didn't lose myself. It changed my view and how I fit into this view…*" "*Expression*" is in there somewhere, because I keep seeing the word "*expression.*" But she says, "*The old me did not die when this left, I was still me.*"

What was gained in transitioning from the earthly realm to spirit was a whole new perspective on things. Not only about life in general, but about the spirits themselves in particular. A combined assessment of the answers tallied up to be something that not only opened up one's mind, but also brought encouragement and hope for the future—a sense of self-nurturing each had lacked while alive on earth. At first glance, it all seems so self-serving, until we take into account that all things in the universe are connected and One—if a single person can reach the pinnacle of excellence, benevolence, and love, it affects all others. This was exemplified in session one, with Michael, the beloved friend of my sitter, Leah:

> He says, "*If you're referring to some notion that the transition,
> the passing from here to there, wipes certain things away from
> you intellectually, no, no, no.*" He says, "*You bring that forward.
> As you continue forward into this realm, you wind up leaving
> more of it behind, so there is a gradual letting go of pretty much
> everything that you no longer want to hold within your being...
> But going from here to there, no, you don't lose who you are.*"
> What is gained? Self-love. He shows that to me in an image.
> He shows me dark and black at the top, light at the bottom after
> the transition. This earth-realm he makes it black and carries it
> into the afterlife. After the Life Review, he gets a newfound
> respect for himself. He says, "*It's not that easy. I had to have
> help from some of the people that were there. It still comes from
> within yourself—they don't give it to you. All they can do is give
> you...tips, clues, and highlights.*"

From this answer, one can surmise that after passing into the spirit
world, those others who have been in spirit for a long time can inspire and
lead the way in letting go of our former earthly lives. But like all things,
the choice of how we evolve into the future is purely our own and is not
necessarily an easy adaptation of releasing the ties that bind us, an indicated by Brandon from session two:

> He says you don't lose anything. And that was one of the...He
> feels really heavy around that. I think that totally has to relate
> to the way of his passing...He wanted to lose all that, but he
> didn't. It wasn't like "*I'm changed now, it's all gone.*" He's saying
> because the emotions...those don't go away. When he got
> over there..."*It's all in my emotions, my emotions...Because this
> did not work...those emotions were still in me when I got here...
> They don't disappear.*" What do you gain? What you gain is
> a perspective, a way of seeing and being that will allow you
> to let go of it. Although he says, "*I haven't completely let go of
> it, but I have...I don't feel so emotional about it anymore.*" He

still retains the memories, but the memories don't affect him as much anymore.

And session four, as Grace's grandmother explained it to me:

> She says, "*I didn't lose anything. In fact, what I gained was a larger perspective on who I had been in my life. That gave me a wider vision of who I was.*" They opened her mind up to...be less critical of herself, to be more open with herself. She says the only thing she lost was the body she left behind, and was thankful to lose it.

Undoubtedly, the Life Review plays a huge role in this process of gaining wisdom, as evidenced by Rose, from session eleven:

> She's making me feel like there were some aspects of her identity that she lost. To me, she's making me feel like it has to do with the need to control everything—because she keeps pounding on a table. "*This was the part of my identity that I lost. I wanted to string everything in and do it to my whim.*"

Of course, Terri was nodding the whole time as I was describing this portrait of her grandmother's personality. Apparently Rose was quite a spitfire in her early years, something I wasn't witness to when I had met her before she passed. I continued with the rush of images and feelings she was giving me:

> She says, "*That part of my identity I lost.*" And then she contrasts that with, "*Because I gained the understanding that it is a cooperative relationship between everybody.*" I think this was the biggest point of the Life Review, in seeing everything and how she affected everybody. It could have been a relationship—swaying back and forth between people versus "*do this, do this.*"

And also from the spirit of Kourtnie's father in session twelve:

He's making me feel like…"*Aspects that I lost? No, I really didn't lose anything.*" What he gained was that sense back in the Life Review of just how magnificent he really was. He just shows that last half of the Life Review… and pulls it out and says, "*Wow, this is me. This is cool.*" He found a newfound personal love for himself; this is what he gained."

Finally, I think Gabi's mother from session thirteen really encapsulated the whole thing. What one loses and then gains, ultimately, is a newfound love for life itself. From the transcript:

The aspect of her identity that she says she lost, was whatever that fear was that kept her depressed for all those decades (before passing). I don't know what her thought processes were or motivations were to have had that …To me it feels like self-criticism… She lost that judgment towards herself. What did she gain? She says a newfound love and respect for life— in the sense that she is living much happier now than when she was here. That has given her a newfound respect that… "*I wish I would have had this back here (on earth) because it would've made things a whole lot better for everybody.*" She now owns that her condition affected other people while she was here… She starts drawing strings off of it and gravitating them toward other people. "*If I were this person I am now while back on earth, I would have spared myself and the other people that were affected. But what's done is done.*" But she gained a new-found respect and love for life. There's actually a lust for life, whereas before there wasn't.

In the end, the personality of a traveling soul remains intact. The attitudes, joys, and even the things one disliked, are still carried forward. But thanks to the Life Review and shedding of the physical world, a whole new perspective is birthed that suggests the end of the physical life will be renewed by a thirst for the new dimension. As I have heard it described elsewhere, when the curtain comes down on one's life on earth, it becomes the opening night on the Other Side—and that's when *real* life begins.

8

Do You Have a New Kind of Body or Are You Without Form?

I had always wondered about this question. If spirits are not bound by space, do they even have a body at all? If so, does that not predispose some kind of "space" being taken up? As revealed to me in the course of *The Afterlife Interviews*, corporeal life and structure is more of a mental phenomenon that is solidified through the frequency of various levels of consciousness. That is, if we think "*solid*," things will be so. Let's face it, in the three-dimensional world in which you and I currently live, science knows that an atom is 99% empty space. Similarly, though we can dive into a pool of water, sometimes that fluid can hit us like it was solid rock given the best belly-flop condition (this was an answer shown to me in the Interviews).

When it came to answering this question, every one of my sitter's deceased friends or relatives claimed to have a new body—and that we on earth would consider it to be *both* solid and malleable were we to be experiencing it ourselves in the spiritual world. Nancy's father from session three had this to say:

> He's got a new kind of body, and he says it's very solid. He beats himself on the abdomen. He's definitely referencing the solidness of the body. He's saying, "*You just don't get it, you just don't get it, but it's solid.*" He shows it…little bubbles of cells and stuff going off, going off, going off…and says, "*This is what*

*you're already doing, you're just in a different zone than I...but
I'm still just as solid as you."*

The mention of "little bubbles" made me think of all the cells and atoms
that currently make up our physique. Sarah's grandfather from session
six had this to say:

> He makes me feel that I definitely have a body. He slams it
> down on the floor and says, "*I have force, I have structure.*"

Fortunately, several of the deceased were willing to give a glimpse as to
the body's fluid nature as well. This is not much different than our earthly
body—where every cell in our body will have died and been replaced
every seven years. That we do not look the same as we did five, ten, or
twenty years ago (nor will we in the future), gives us an awareness of our
earthly body's fluidity. The body in the afterlife, however, is not bound
by Time, so the notion of decay or aging becomes moot. The frequency or
speed at which the spiritual realm vibrates is immensely quicker than our
own, according to those spirits who have come through to talk about such
things. Apparently, this rapidity of the energy on the Other Side in some
ways inhibits disease and decay. Moreover, the primacy of consciousness
and the power of one's thoughts have more of an observable reality due
to this frequency or speed; for on earth, our thoughts do influence and
create reality and experience, yet through the prism of Time—a slower
moving process indeed. Plus, without Time being the harbinger of decay,
the deceased can remain free of the earthly condition of growing old, as
expressed by Grace's grandmother from session four:

> She's taken on a form. She takes the image of the body and
> sucks it back thirty or forty years, making her appearance
> younger.

From the spirit of Cynthia's father in session five:

> He would characterize it as a body, but he's very much aware
> of the fluid nature of it. In a sense, it's not different from your

body now with cells and atoms…It's just a different frequency range. And he says, *"It's going much faster, much faster,"* and attributing this speed as to why the spiritual body doesn't get sick, ill, or corrupt…because the energy is moving so much quicker, as if to keep it unsusceptible to certain conditions.

And from Rose in session eleven:

She's making me feel like she has adopted a new body. She makes me feel heaviness to it, as if to say, *"I have a form, I have a body that I have adopted and accepted. And I'm back in my twenties. I'm not the frail old woman I was. I'm back in my twenties."* And she says, *"I still like to drink."* Did she drink?

Terri replied that Rose didn't drink a lot in her adult years, but there were plenty of wild stories of her grandmother's youth about how she would go overboard with all of her drinking. Apparently, she couldn't hold her liquor then, but now on the Other Side she made me feel like she was doing some indulging with the new body.

Being a medium is to be a conduit of information from spirit. In order to do that, I have to completely focus in the Now moment and just let whatever messages come through. I make no effort to remember or retain the information—rather, I just want to process the information and get it out. And since I was recording and transcribing these sessions, I had less of an inclination to remember what was being said from one spirit to the next. Nevertheless, a few souls described the makeup of this new body in similar terms. It wasn't until I started to review the answers to my questions that I realized how incredible these descriptions were. In a way, I took them as being complimentary to one another. That more than one spirit described the body in similar terms (as you'll see in the following questions as well), was quite a wondrous occurrence to me—and these sittings were several months apart. Remember what Nancy's father had said:

He shows it…little bubbles of cells and stuff going off, going off, going off…

It was this description of little bubbles that kept popping up, similar to what Cynthia's father had described:

> He shows me a really dense bottle of soda pop. You get all the carbonated bubbles, and he says, "*Throw in another few million of those bubbles and see how dense that gets.*"

For some spirits, they understood the body as being a projection from their own focus of consciousness and were using it simply for the purpose of identification. This was what was told to me by the spirit of Marti's mother from session ten:

> She says in some respects, she doesn't have to have a body, but she prefers to project one...I think this is more for other people's benefit than her own. She makes it very...I want to say *fluid*...meaning I think she can change it up at will. She's making me feel like...She says, "*It's really good for dad, your dad, to have this body for him to look at here.*" I really think she's just doing it for other people's benefit and not necessarily her own.

And from Debbie's father in session seven, who added this:

> He's saying, "*I couldn't stand being without form.*" He stands up straight and sucks it in. "*Yeah, I've got form,*" and he sucks it in.

Gabi's mother from session thirteen came forward with this to say:

> She can't fathom being without a form...Her identity is wrapped up with a form. She says, "*It's not much different from what you have now. But due to the nature of energetic dynamics, it doesn't turn into a corpse.*" She says, "*From your standpoint, you'd see it as pure energy,*" but aside from that, because of how things work, you can touch it, you can slam it, you can do all that...So it still has touch to it, oomph to it. But because it's vibrating at a different frequency from you and I,

we can't experience it that way. She says, *"Once you get over here, you realize that your body is an energy frequency, and you just can't get disease. The process of life/death/decay...just doesn't exist, because everything is alive. It just produces and creates...produces and creates."* She says, *"You own the feel of the body...You own the course of the body..."* She says, *"Why would you make it dense and hurtful when you know you can have it be open and free? You understand that you have direct control over how this works."* Has something to do with how fast everything is moving. She says, *"Because of how fast we're moving, there's no need for sustenance to maintain it; there's no need for anything to make it operate."* She says, *"It's not a battery or engine you need to put gas into, because it is just energy and life in motion."*

And finally, from Diane from session fourteen:

She says, *"Oh, Honey, now I can suck it in and I have big boobs."*

My sitter, Heidi, busted up laughing. Apparently Diane was not only cheeky with her quips, but also quite weight-challenged while on earth. Diane continued:

She's laughing about that...She gets to have a model body now. She is showing me Jessica Rabbit. *"I get to have this now."* She makes me feel like she definitely has form...she puts solidarity behind it. She makes me feel like it's a very fluid form, *"But if I want to feel something, I am going to feel it like you feel it."* She says, *"I understand it is an energetic matrix of the body."* She says, *"It's just what your body is now, a tapestry of atoms and such."* Same thing over there, just on a different frequency. She says your physical body works within the laws and construct of the physical world you live in...She says, *"Take it to the next level, I am now in a different energy environment, so my body works with the laws and frequency of this new environment. It's a parallel explanation."*

It appears that when you live with the concept or identity of a body in the physical world, this concept carries forward into the afterlife. However, the new body is recognized as being chosen from the mind of the personality—height, weight, look, age, et cetera. Because the frequency of energy in which the souls of the Other Side reside is so much quicker than the slow density of earth, the physical and biological laws of which we are familiar seem to disappear. The decay or otherwise destruction of the body and its organs do not appear possible from the energetic frequency domain of the Other Side, which leaves everyone quite free to be seen as the eternal beings they most assuredly are.

If There Is a New Body, Are There Any Clues You Can Give Us as to the Nature of What the Body is Like in the Afterlife?

Many of the responses to this question naturally turned out to be more or less extensions of the last. Again, references to the structure of the body being visually akin to carbonated water were given. As before, I think it was another analogy of how our current body on earth is quite similar— with atoms and molecules being representative of bubbling carbonation. Everyone who came through in the sessions stressed how malleable their new bodies were, and how that fluidity was tied to their thinking. From Michael in session one:

> He says it's very malleable. *"You can think things through,"* whatever that means. I think he's referring to…Was he scrawny while he was here?

My sitter, Leah, replied in the affirmative.

> He says, *"If you wanted to have the nice toned muscles that you didn't have, you can get them just by thinking about them. I can change my appearance at my will."*

Then from Brandon, who also gave an interesting glimpse of possibilities when it came to the absence of gravity:

It's very, very light. His reference is: it's like being on the moon. You can jump and do flips and gravity isn't going to pull you down. It's that sort of thing…It's very open to what you want to do. He's giving me a Superman reference, as if to say, "*I'm bulletproof. This is like Teflon, it can't be scratched, burned, harmed, or anything. It's like I'm Superman.*"

As mentioned previously, the visual of bubbles was a recurrent theme, as revealed from these excerpts from a couple sessions:

She's saying…for you…it's little particles bubbling around one another all the time…There are so many, and it creates an illusion of form, yet it's something you can pass through. You can have solidity when you want it, from their point-of-view.

He's showing me…a glass of soda with the bubbles, and he's running it over his face. He's showing me his mustache coming in and going out. He's saying it's energy you can manipulate at your whim to get the image you want.

The predominant information that came from this question was how the spiritual body was made of light—and that its vibration was very fast. The spirits suggested that this higher frequency was related to the lack of disease that "seems" to attack the earthly body. From their perspective on the Other Side, they also acknowledged they were responsible for the new light body's construction. Here's what Grace's grandmother had to say from session four:

There's something about light she's talking about…It's light, it's light…She's giving me an ocean reference…You can dip your hand in it, and yet you can slap it and it's hard.

And from Cynthia's father in session five:

And he's making some kind of comment about light…light being connected to the body, but I'm not getting what the connection is. Did he have invasive surgery?

Cynthia confirmed that he did have some major invasive surgery.

> He keeps showing me the big cuts and using this to say, "*This does not happen here.*" This is where he gives me the light reference. "*Because the body is made of light, we don't have to cut it like a piece of fabric.*" And this speed…speed is a very important message.

And from session six, with Sarah's Muslim grandfather:

> He comes over here, as if to say, "*Here's my body*" and he blasts light out of it. He says, "*This goes forward from within…*" So he's referencing that he's aware that the body which he has comes from his own being. It's not something that is put on like clothing, it's something he generates. He's saying, "*Because I think this way, I get to control how this feels and what happens to this.*" He's saying, part of our problem down here on earth, we don't understand how our thoughts work in the body. He's making me feel like, down here on earth since it's a much slower moving environment, slower moving process, our thoughts—because they are slow—don't immediately affect the body in a mass sense. But he's saying, "*Diseases and stuff you feel down here, come from your own mind and nowhere else; it just sometimes takes a little time for bad thoughts to show up on your body.*" But on the Other Side, he keeps snapping his fingers, quick. So when you realize your thoughts quickly result in your body, you are able to maintain healthy thoughts, healthy mind, and healthy body.

Marti's mother from session ten was also very insistent on how the body was a thought-form:

> She says it has everything to do with your thinking, with your thoughts, with your mental energy. It's something you project

outward from your mind. She must have been a deep thinker when she was alive...She just seems like, she's not taking anything for granted and is paying close attention to how things operate and how they work.

Which was backed up several times throughout the sessions, including what Rose had said to her granddaughter, Terri:

She's saying it's not a set structure—that it's not a defined body, like in the corporeal laws of physics. She's saying, think of it like a wire mesh—how the mesh is so flexible and able to be molded and that things can go through it. That's what the body is like for her. It's not something that can be slammed into a wall and broken.

This difference between the energetic nature of the Other Side and the slow density of earth really came to the forefront of Diane's response to this question. Her background in science really came through in the way she projected images and impressions into my consciousness. She provided an excellent explanation of the differences between the energetic and earthly physical forms:

She is saying for both bodies—whether on earth or the Other Side—it's the mind and the way you think which affects both. She says the body on earth is much grosser...because here there are organs and tissues to move stuff...it's part of the environment and how to operate...On the Other Side, since it's not a physical environment in the sense that we understand physicality, there are no organs to the body...but it's still acknowledged of how the mind projects it. She is showing me an image of the body, and then she shows me a whirlpool of energy through the structure. *"This is me controlling my body with my thoughts."* She says you still do this on earth, but you're also dealing with organs and tissues, because there are earthly components for how that body is to survive in the environment that it requires those organs and tissues. But on the Other

Side, the body is a projection of your energy and your mind, it doesn't require the same kind of construction.

In a nutshell, the combination of thoughts along with light and frequency gives rise to the spiritual form a personality takes. Because the nature of the Other Side is on a different frequency of vibration, if we were to apply certain laws of physics and dynamics we would discover that such laws do not work in the same ways as on earth; this includes even the body. Different environments—different realities—naturally give rise to different manifestations. To me, the most profound answer came from Debbie's father, who gave a great visual of separation between earth and the spiritual realm and how it related to the body:

> He says, "*On earth, you have organs and stuff that have to work together in order to function. Here, there are no physical organs to make you move...it's all...*" He's using the word "*harmony*" in the context of sound...it's harmony, it's wholeness, it's vibration...a different kind of matrix. "*It doesn't require organs to work together to make it work. It's a different kind of construction.*" He's saying, "*Much of the human body deals with ingestion and elimination, processes and processing—because of the nature of the environment. Here we don't have to deal with that, so it's different...It's an energy body versus tubes and stuff.*"

10

Do You Have Any Kind of Physical or Bodily Health Issues to Deal With in the Afterlife?

Again, this question became an extension of the last, with the answers revealing information about how thoughts form and impact the body, the nature of the body's energy in the afterlife, and interestingly, the concept of illness from those who have gone on into the next reality.

It has always been assumed that in the afterlife there would be no such thing as bodily health issues; however, no one has officially and directly asked that question (to my knowledge). So my purpose for the inquiry was to hear fourteen different times the same answer for consensus. And indeed, in all cases I received a resounding *"No!"* to the presence of bodily "dis-ease" in the afterlife. Fortunately, the spirits were willing to offer a bit more, carrying on the conversation created by the previous two questions regarding the energetic body. From Sarah's grandfather in session six:

> He's making me feel like, in terms of maladies, no. But he keeps showing me blasting light, blasting light…As if to say, for awhile there, he experimented with his body. When he realized that he could *"construct"* with his mind his form, he spent some time constructing. He didn't automatically choose something; he played with the light. *"When an opportunity came up to construct a body, I played with it. There's never an in-between state, you are always something. You just know at that point, your consciousness and your being are intact; they're not going*

anywhere. You can hold onto your sense of self and create these possibilities with your energy for what you want to look like." He's also saying, *"You do have some control over facial features,"* but he's also making me feel like, you have a certain energy as a personality and it is that which gets translated into the form; so you may have similar eyes or cheek structure, but you still have a lot of leeway between things—height, weight, age—you can play with all of that. *"Whether or not you want to be bald or have hair, you can play with that."*

Marti's mother in session ten added to the topic:

> She's saying the body is very fine energy...very fine energy... It doesn't get disease. She's making me feel like disease is ... it has to do with a physical body process. She's making me feel like that since the body vibrates at such a slower rate on earth, there are components that allow for an increase in disease in the body. She's making me feel like the energy here (in heaven) is so much finer, and the vibratory rate is so much better that the body can't get disease like it does on earth.

Interestingly, when one gets used to having constant physical pain in life, there is some anticipation of that pain carrying over into the new body, mainly because of the mental habit of feeling it. What a relief it was for Rose when she finally hit the Other Side, as she described in session eleven:

> And she had a lot going on through the upper parts, too, correct? I'm like, from the belt, all the way up.

Her granddaughter, Terri, confirmed multiple problems that had wracked her grandmother's whole upper body.

> She's like, *"When I was here, when I first took on the new body, I was still expecting to feel..."* When she first arrived, it took her a while to get used to the idea that she didn't have those

problems. She had gotten so used to having them and thinking about them, of being aware of them, that she was like, "*What do you mean I don't have them?*" It took her awhile to get used to the idea that she didn't have those issues anymore.

This was also a similar reaction according to Gabi's mother from session thirteen, who had passed earlier in the year. Part of the pain of her condition had been that she was filling up with fluids, so much so that her belly had protruded unnaturally, to the point that her belly button was literally popping out. I didn't know this at the time of the sitting, but when she answered this question, the visual she had given me couldn't have been more accurate:

> She had a lot of abdominal issues, too. She is saying "*I am so happy to be over this.*" It had to be like a rock in the belly... She's showing me a bowling ball, that her abdomen looked like a bowling ball. She says she is so happy she doesn't have to deal with that anymore.

As alluded to in the previous questions, the new body is composed of light. This was repeated over and over again throughout the series. Nancy's father in session three described it like this:

> He's going back to the light in, light out thing. He's saying, "*Now comes my spiritual side.*" Since going over there, he's really gotten into this whole light thing. It's all about the light. It's all about the warmth of the light. It's about the "*interpenetration*" of light. It really got his curiosity up, when he finally got relaxed into this new environment...the properties of light. Did he have a bit of a scientific background?

According to Nancy, technically her father was not a scientist, but he always thought in a very analytical and left-brained way. He had always reminded her of thinking and acting like a scientist. He went on:

> He's making me feel "science" with it. Part of this thing with the

light has the science behind it, but I think what captured him was the actual feeling of it—and the feeling inside...and the emotion that gets attached with it.

But ultimately, how we hold onto our thoughts and feelings appeared to be the greatest message that those on the Other Side really wished to relate when it came to the concept of bodily health issues and disease. From the spirit of Michael in session one:

> He's saying..."*I understand now why people on earth get sick. It has to do with how your thoughts and your energy affect your organism.*" But there, in the spirit realm, he's telling me they have a much better grasp of what's going on up here (in the head, mentally and emotionally) so they can somehow make— he's using the word "*orchestration*"—you're able to orchestrate the energy better..."*While you're here on earth, all this stuff affects one thing and the other. You can't necessarily isolate your thinking and your feelings from everything else in your body at all. It all represents itself.*" He says that there (in spirit) you have a much better grasp of the mechanics of thought, feeling, of how impressions inform the mold. You would never get a disease over there in the body, because you are aware of how your thoughts are creative in that respect. So, one of the things you can do over there is work through that without having to worry about it affecting your body.

And another interesting perspective from Debbie's father in session seven:

> He says, "*Only what I care to deal with in my mind.*" He says the body is affected by concentrated thought. "*Willy-nilly thoughts don't affect the energy so much as a concentrated one.*" He says, "*We're so much more aware of our vibration of thought, the way we think...*"

As soon as I delivered this message, I started to wonder that if one can think a certain thing for many years and have it impact one's physical body, does the same process happen over there on the Other Side? If a spirit were to think along a certain line over extended periods of time (for whatever time is to them), would it impact his or her body in some way? Debbie's father responded:

> He says, "*Well, we're much more aware here, with how the mind interacts with the body. It would take a good concentration of thought.*" He makes me feel like, it's an intuitive knowing, or you've got guides…something helps to keep you in a higher level of thinking than what we've got here on earth.

The most intriguing response came from session five, where my sitter, Cynthia, was so excited to be hearing from her father. On many occasions, we often hear how the spirits of our loved ones are watching over us. Apparently, there are others besides our immediate family who still take an interest in our earthly lives. Cynthia's father spoke of those spirits in the afterlife who were physicians in their earthly incarnations and had still retained an active interest in earthly medicine despite their new disease-free reality. Since medicine and the nature of illness were passions for these souls while alive on earth, they have continued to study them on the Other Side. Their intention, it seems, is to have the information one day return to earth, either as an inspiration or gifted insight to be realized by a reincarnational self:

> …And he's also tacking on something about people in spirit that were once physicians and doctors…Once they get over there, they start taking a look at deeper relational things with the body, to better understand how…corporate the structure is? Not sure if that's the right word. 'C-o-r' is part of the sound, but it's a long word like corporation, referring to how the body works. He's making me feel like there are former earthly physicians over there, that in studying how this light body works, are attempting to understand certain bio-functions in order to hopefully…reincarnate back again with some of this knowledge that they could then put into current earthly standards. They want to take some of this knowledge

back down and bring it to humanity. He's saying they're not trying to give it to physicians on earth through dreams or inspirational material; they want to bring it back down themselves because they're going to have a better chance at retaining the knowledge, rather than trying to present it in an inspirational manner. There's complexity to it.

So it appears that due to the frequency of vibration and thought, a new body is generated by the mind of the soul; yet this form is purely for representation and not necessity. Similarly, the energetic body is not perceived as a "prison" or "cage" from which the soul must live out its eternal days. Rather, the soul can shift, change, or alter this image or appearance by intention alone, by manipulating light or other energy fields that must be emitted to create the form. An intriguing prospect for our future selves—goodbye to wrinkles, pimples, aches and pains, or any of that other dis-ease we spend so much money on in today's world to get away from.

11

Do You Age or Do You Get to Choose Your Appearance?

The answer to this seemed like a no-brainer after hearing the responses from the previous questions. Indeed, every one of my sitters' friends or relatives all reported that they did get to choose their appearance. Interestingly, this choice can also be altered; that is, once you choose an appearance, you are not stuck with that image for the rest of eternity. In some cases, certain appearances harkened back to certain times in one's life, and being able to take on that form may be therapeutic, as it was for Debbie's father:

> He's making me feel like, for a while, he chose to be a little kid. He's making me feel like, "*I needed to get that energy out,*" that it was stifled. He didn't get to be a kid…so he took some time and was a kid for awhile before assuming the adult appearance. Here…he says to me, "*I took on two different forms for awhile. Being a kid was definitely one of them.*"

Several of the deceased were adamant that aging by way of history simply was not a factor on the Other Side. To them, growth was measured not by the passing of seasons, but by how they developed psychologically, emotionally, and ultimately, holistically. From Sarah's grandfather in session six:

You don't age. You get to choose your appearance. He says, *"You get to grow...in terms of knowledge and experience and that could be considered aging...But not aging in terms of your body going through these changes. No, no."*

From session nine, with the spirit of Teri K.'s brother:

He's making me feel like he is a lot older (than he was when he passed), but physically, no. He would consider his age connected to the wisdom that he's gained.

And from Marti's mother in session ten:

She's really making me feel like the whole age-time thing has no meaning. Zero. She says, *"When you get over here, you'll forget that time exists."*

And finally, Rose, Terri's grandmother:

She's saying, *"I get to choose my appearance. And by golly, it's nice to be young again."* And she's making me feel like when it comes to the idea of aging, like through the course of Time, no. *"We don't have to deal with that here."'* She says that's the other bonus with being here: *"I don't have to grow old."*

Michael, the first spirit in the interviews, told me he had been away for so long that the concept of aging was a foreign concept to his consciousness! This is how it came out in the transcript:

He says you get to choose your appearance. Age is completely...He's been gone for long while, hasn't he? He says age is something he can't even relate to anymore.

Gabi's mother made a point to her lovely daughter about her self-image, which totally surprised me. Gabi is a healthy, fit mother—not someone in my eyes who had any issues with weight. Yet when her mother answered this question, she was blatant about Gabi's misgivings which apparently haunted her daughter for many years:

> She says, "*I get to choose my appearance. And that you bitch too much about your weight!'*

Gabi's mouth metaphorically hit the floor when her mother came through with this message. She gasped a resounding "Yes!"

> She's saying you will get to stop worrying about how your weight looks. And you will finally be happy!

Heidi's friend, Diane, gave me a nice little zinger as her answer:

> She says, "*Honey, when it comes to age, I am eternal.*"

So even though we are subject to the course of Time on earth and what that does to our bodies, not only is the new energetic body free of diseases, it is also free from the effects of chronological aging. So if you'd like to go back to being a kid again, feel free! When Time has no bearing on your appearance, you become the master of your age in the visual sense and eternity whole-heartedly supports it.

12

When Leaving the Earthly Existence Were You Automatically Given Wisdom or Answers to the Nature of Life and Existence That You Didn't Have While You Were Alive on Earth? Was Knowledge Instantly Bestowed upon You? If So, What Did You Learn?

It's easy to assume that when someone dies and transitions to heaven—and if you can theoretically sit next to God or dwell in His temple—that some amazing new knowledge about how the universe works would be granted. Once the limits of the physical mind and body have been discarded, it does stand to reason that the newfound freedom from Time and Space would reveal eternal truths so spectacular that they could make your head spin!

In truth, the alteration from earth-life to the spiritual realm does give a whole new perspective on how the former physical existence progressed in terms of events, but unfortunately doesn't give you the keys to all wisdom. At the time I was designing the questions for the book (and before I had my first session even scheduled) I knew this question had to be asked. I approached it from the perspective of *"If the workings of the universe are a cloud of fog to me, then when I die does that cloud lift?"* The responses from the sessions were profound...and quite reasonable.

Right away, it became clear there was no way the vastness of the entire universe could be comprehended easily or quickly, especially after a short span of a single lifetime on earth. That's like trying to teach calculus to a three-year-old, comparatively. Nonetheless, however, if a three-year-old can learn to add or subtract, that doesn't mean calculus isn't out of the question sometime in the child's future. Apparently, the greater universe and the knowledge contained therein works in a similar manner. And like the Life Review process, new knowledge and wisdom is on a personal level, based on interests and experiences. Definitely, we would all like sacred universal knowledge to open up and download into our consciousness when we die, to finally "understand what all this is about." But, as the spirits told me, that is not really the case. From the spirit of Michael in session one:

> He's saying, *"As in someone just waving a wand and ding! No. It's like anything, it's a matter of how you change perspective."* He says, *"When you're there on earth you have one perspective; when you get out you have another perspective, but it is your own perspective. The universe isn't granting you anymore wisdom than what you have."* It builds slowly and in little pockets based on your perceptions and observations, is what he's showing me. *"Because you are in this mold here on earth, you are predisposed—based on the limitations of existing reality—to come up with certain ideas and thoughts. But once you are out of that..."* He's showing the Other Side being like a box that goes over the three-dimensional realms and says, *"Okay, this kind of expands...it incorporates the physical, but it also shows you a little bit beyond that. That does give you a little bit different perspective."* He also says it doesn't make you a messiah or Moses.

What this answer suggested was that universal wisdom doesn't just appear, but being in the new environment does grant a whole new perspective on things. However, that new perspective is still very personal; that is, it's a viewpoint that is still filtered through the individual's mental framework of beliefs and attitudes. In other words, no two people share the same view of a single event. From Grace's grandmother in session four:

She says, *"The only knowledge about existence of life that I got was my own...my own...It pertained to my own life."* She's saying there are schools of thought which surround us about what is supposed to happen when you pass away—certain events, certain ideas, certain knowledge being granted you...She says no, it doesn't work that way. *"Hierarchy"* is the word I'm hearing...There are certain belief systems that have a hierarchy that you bought into before you passed away. She says, *"That formation, that hierarchy doesn't exist...It's just a belief system that people have while they're alive."* And then in this hierarchy, there is this expectation of gaining knowledge or wisdom of God or the universe that is supernatural or above the norm. She says, *"No, that doesn't happen."* You will gain some wisdom and some knowledge by the nature of the environment being different from earth, but she says your life is the context of the vastness of knowledge that comes through to you, it is through your life...so you're not going to get a direct pipeline to God. She says that comes later through your experiences... through your presence of mind. When she says that, she draws a cord, and references the movement of Time...as if to say, as you journey through life with presence of mind, that is your cord to the wisdom of God...It comes through experiences that you attain.

From Terri K.'s brother in session nine:

He's showing me...Things weren't bestowed. But he's showing me that, while we're on earth, we're in an optical illusion. He shows me an image and shifts it...*"When you cross, it changes the direction of things to such a degree that you go, 'Oh, it's really like this,' that you couldn't see at the time."* It's a shift in perspective that opens up new ideas and thoughts. He's making me feel like...to him, it's not so mysterious as it once was. He's making me feel like it's not as enigmatic as we're making it, in terms of how one relates to the other and how it all evolved.

And from Kourtnie's father in my twelfth session:

> He's making me feel like, *"No, the kingdom of heaven was not given me."* Knowledge that was bestowed was…personal, is how he's making me feel. He wants to attach the knowledge to himself. It was self-realization. He says, *"To come out here and reach the stars and get information—it wasn't like that. There was a better overall sense of community connection with everything else. There wasn't this huge opening of the mind and getting all this stuff dropped in it."*

Several of the spirits spoke about how the new knowledge they gained was very specific to their own needs. Whatever issues were plaguing them on earth, when they reached the Other Side, this new perspective from the eternal abode helped them deal with their concerns. But aside from that, great universal knowledge and wisdom were not handed them, though the spirits acknowledged that their own evolution was the key to enlightenment, as evidenced by the transcription here of Nancy's father from session three:

> He's giving me two answers…He's saying, *"In the grand overall scheme, no, I didn't receive universal knowledge, but rather in the minor scheme of my own individual self and how…and how I degraded things…"* How he judged things, he got a new perspective on all that. He shows me looking down at himself and seeing bars he put in place to limit…And it's like…*"What I just learned being over here took those right out."*
> He is saying, *"You wear limitations like a suit. And until you realize how you look…You wear the same suit for many, many years without realizing there's a whole different wardrobe out there."* For him, the process revealed the suit he was wearing, and he decided to take it off and look at some different apparel.

And when it came to the spirit of Brandon who had committed suicide, he offered this as his answer to receiving universal wisdom from on-high:

He's making feel like, *"No, no, nobody came down and gave me the secrets of the universe."* He's saying it's so vastly important that each person makes the strides in his or her own mind and being, *"lessons...make for...the experience."* He's making me feel like the larger experience is a result of the individual lessons and the individual things. In addressing what we would consider the individual or smaller issues contributes to understanding and getting a better impression of the larger.

Like some of the spirits that came after him, Brandon is stressing that the experiences throughout life are the key to accessing the wisdom of existence. Though he may have cut his time on earth short, this answer clearly demonstrated a learned wisdom since arriving on the Other Side. This was restated by Cynthia's father in session five:

He makes me feel like he gained knowledge, but it was... because he was kind of already thinking this stuff while he was on earth...He got better clarification on his thoughts. He shows me that, *"I had a perception...and when I got here and I got looking at these things I used to wonder about...I got more knowledge, but it was all in relation to the areas I was interested in."* He's making me feel like, *"There is information out here, but since it was not stuff I was interested in, I didn't automatically get all this information downloaded into me...It's still stuff I have to go and input myself, be a part of; it's not instantly downloaded."*

The notion of being able to gain additional insight into predisposed areas of study was echoed emphatically by Diane in session fourteen. Her hobbies while on earth were hiking and studying nature, as she had the mind of a scientist and heart of an explorer. Here's what she gave me when it came to receiving God's wisdom:

She is making me feel like, *"I did gain a new wisdom,"* but she keeps it very personal. Because she was very much into...the earth, natural, and physical sciences...That was her focus...that is what came into her awareness over there—how it was really shifted from looking at it one way to looking at it in a different way. That was the change she got. Outside of that, nothing much more.

She's showing me a biodome over a city and somebody opening it up to the universe and saying, *"That doesn't happen. It's not like the biodome is removed and you're given all the answers."* She says, *"You will get what you are asking for in the amounts you are capable of understanding. There are more layers and levels to learn and graduate to."* She says, *"You can't look at the events of your life that you have to go through as shit…In order to fully understand and appreciate it at the end, you have to go through the steps, otherwise, you would not get it. So, you can't look at this as a painful journey, you've got to look at it as the steps necessary to fully appreciate it when you reach the top."*

When new knowledge comes, if it doesn't come from the simple fact of existing from a new point of view, then it's not given in one big fell swoop according to Sarah's grandfather in session six:

He's making me feel like, *"It would've been a whole lot easier if knowledge was instantly bestowed upon me…No, wisdom isn't instantly given you…but you are 'walked through on the course.'"* He's making a reference to…course…education…something like that. There's something there that you go through, little by little…He's making me feel like, they're only going to give you what they think you can handle. He's making me feel like, *"Universal wisdom is too great to throw on a man as soon as he dies. It's too great, it's too massive; it's unfathomable. They will only give you what you can handle. And it's only what you really need in order to get yourself moving."* But once you are there, and he's referencing once you've left that transition space and get to where you're going, as soon as you hit that spot, a whole array of stuff opens up for you, for you to explore; but it's totally your choice as to what the ideas and explorations are.

Nobody hands you a textbook and says, *"Okay, it's time for you to learn this."*

Nevertheless, new information—though not universal, per se—does move the soul forward and invites wisdom, as these deceased relatives of my sitters revealed, starting with M.G.'s mother from session eight:

> She makes me feel like she did gain a little more wisdom…And it has to do with interrelated connectedness to everything. She's making me feel like, *"It's not like I went from Point A to Point B…It's more like…"* It's not even wiser…*"I'm aware, I have experience, I have conditioned awareness."* And this would have been the angle of her guru when he passed. There's this sense to me of her relationship still being with him, that he is still acting in the role of mentor. He was able to take what he had learned since he'd passed, and gently kind of bring her up to speed, although he's still learning. And she says, *"It's not just me, there are others."* So there must be others that passed from a similar group that he was the focus of…And some of them were higher up…I don't know how these groups were designed. She is showing me a hierarchy of the group…and some of his higher ups are also there and they are also continuing to do some of the same style of how they did things. But that's only by awareness, meaning, *"We know we don't have to do it this way, but this is how we like to do it. So this is how we go about doing our learning and continuing…"* *"Progression"* is definitely the word she wants to get across.

M.G.'s mother clearly demonstrated in her answer that the evolution of her knowledge was being facilitated by the way she loved to learn: through the interaction of her guru and his group. So not only was she learning by the predisposed nature of her interests, she was doing it in the manner she wished to achieve it!

For some, however, the manner of experience didn't matter in how they gained newfound knowledge in the areas they were interested. In Rose's case, the experiences she remembered from life on earth—when turned around in the spirit realm for review—gave her some enlightenment on the issues that had plagued her:

> She's making me feel like the biggest thing she learned was the value of communicating in relationships. And quite honestly, she's backing that up with saying, *"That's why my marriages failed..."* That was the biggest lesson for her when she finally got over there and went through everything. When looking at it all in retrospect, she started saying to herself: *"Oh, it could've been like this. Oh, communication. That's what it's about."*
>
> She's making me feel like *"knowledge bestowed"* takes on a very personal quality. It's going to be selective to your personal attributes. Any kind of, like, Universal-God knowledge, if that's not what you were focused on while you were here on earth and not what you were driving toward, they're not going to drop it on you when you get there. She says it's very tailored to your specific needs, your specific environment.

Gabi's mother in session thirteen described it like this:

> She is screaming, *"Hallelujah, I realized I had choices."* She must have felt like she was always a victim of circumstances, or things always happened *to* her. But there is this big hallelujah of *"I have the say! I have the say!"* And you know what, she doesn't complain about *"God, had I done this back in life."* She's let a lot of earth life go. She accepts that she has her power over there and can live her life the way she chooses...She says, *"I'm not just choosing, I'm directing it!"*

For some on the Other Side, when we hear what they have learned, we cannot help but think that some universal knowledge and wisdom had been granted, such as what was delivered by Marti's mother from session ten:

> She keeps pulling energy out of her head and curls it back around and brings it back into herself, as if to say, *"Okay,*

everything that you experience out there in life, starts from within you, it goes out, and then it comes back in for your perception." And she actually spells the word *"responsible"* around this energy that you put out and then bring back. She says, *"You're responsible for this. You've got to own your life, it's your projection. It's your energy that projects and persists and comes back to you."* She's definitely emphatic that your energy is like a battery that juices reality... It's a battery that juices how your life ends up taking its form. Experiences come from your energy, is what she's showing me. She wants to cut off this idea that there's another arm coming in and doing things for you or forcing you to do things outside of your will. She wants to cut it off and say, *"That's not how it works, that's not how it happens. There is no outside force coming in and directing things outside of your own energy."'* Nothing is invalidating your battery is the sense that I'm getting.

So an instantaneous download of new knowledge turning our loved ones into "know all and see all" deities is really quite a misconception. Rather, it seems some new perspectives on the deceased's own unique life path is granted as a result of having to see through a different lens of reality. In that sense, there is new knowledge which might grow into wisdom, but chances are, our deceased loved ones still couldn't tell us how gravity works or why a bat uses sonar to "see" instead of their eyes. This doesn't mean such answers aren't available, it just means that all knowledge and wisdom will be person-specific. But what it also implies— and this is profound—is that we too, while still on earth, have the same innate ability within our souls to open our eyes and expand our minds to better "know" God; that is, if we can get past our own clouded thinking.

How Do You Communicate with Others? Do You Talk or is It Telepathy? What About Physical Things Such as Dancing or Making Love—Are You Able to Do Those Things in the Afterlife?

I know, I know. This is really two questions rolled up into one. My point was to discover what earth-like interactions between people in the spirit world were like. Communication has many forms besides just talking—we all know how much bodily movement, connection, and interaction can send messages—the greatest being the act of making love. But because it does "sound" like a two-part question, many of the spirits chose to answer it in that fashion.

So let's begin with the first question and simply rephrase it as "How is verbal communication achieved? Do you talk or is it telepathy?" The following are a series of excerpts from the sessions. Let's start with the spirit of Michael from session one:

> How do you communicate with others… *"That's the other thing that's really different here,"* he says. *"You don't have to talk. It's as if the message is carried on the wind."*

Grace's grandmother from session four shared this with me:

> The voice is not needed, is what she's showing. *"We don't use voice, we don't use language."*

Terri's grandmother, Rose, put it like this:

> She's showing me that language is not an issue there. What
> she does when it comes to language, she completely shuts her
> mouth...and keeps her tongue still and the information just
> goes. It's like telepathy.

And from Gabi's mother in session thirteen:

> She says communication is inside—it's inner, it's interior. You
> don't have to move a mouth and vocalize. She says that down
> here on earth, because of the way energy works, there has to be
> that vibration in the air for the ears; where over there, since it's
> not physical like it is on earth, it's more energetic..."*energetic*"
> is my word...it just doesn't require the same medium of sound
> to stimulate the eardrums, because there are no eardrums...
> it's all interior.

What became even more fascinating to my sitters and me was how the
deceased described the communication process. They admitted that voice
wasn't needed, but were then willing to go on and describe just how it felt
and how talking could be perceived—at least symbolically. [Incidentally,
the process of communication has been slowly revealed to us in the
Washington State Ghost Society, as we have asked the spirits during the
course of investigations to describe how their "normal" communication
process works by using a combination of psychic reception by Society
mediums and EVPs (electronic voice phenomena) captured on audio
recording devices. With this research, we have postulated a reasonable
picture of how a message is sent and received.] Many spirits had
something to say on this point. A clear description is given by Nancy's
father in session three:

> He says it's a oneness. It's a oneness. As if to say, it's just a
> knowing, you don't have to verbally say anything; you just
> know. It's like, your body just all of a sudden grasps whatever
> it is that's being communicated.

Grace's grandmother from session four expanded the image:

> There is an instantaneous knowing of what is being offered as communication. She says you feel it, you have to feel it. *"That's your key…"* Up here, in the mind…will come into play when it's necessary, but you have to feel it first before it will engage the mind.

From Cynthia's father in session five:

> He goes *"poof"* as if to say, your body just knows what the other person is saying. He says because everything is such fast-moving energy, things move so quickly, and this contributes to how this information works over there. He says, *"When you drop down into your place…"* You get into the nature of speech, where it's air coming up through the larynx, vibrating and making sound; he makes me feel like this is a very archaic, slow process, which is what you get when you are in a slow-moving matter environment—it just doesn't move fast enough for the way things generally should be processed. He makes me feel like the way he communicates now is so natural, that to communicate the way we do, it's archaic to him.

From M.G.'s mother in session eight:

> *"Communication is all inward,"* she says. She shows me the body and a light that blows out like a bulb. She's making me feel like, when somebody communicates, the closest we can get is telepathy, but it's not something that enters the mind, it's something that enters the body…And you just know what it is the other person is trying to communicate…

My wife's friend, Diane, explained it like this:

> She says it's more than telepathy. She keeps coming back to the face, as if to say it hits you in the face and then you get the

whole "*schmoo.*" It's more than words, because you get the whole image and feeling...You just know what it is that is being conveyed. Not just the data...but the feeling behind it, too. She says you get the whole wave of communication energy, the whole thing. You get the whole *quantity* of the information, so there is no guesswork or interpretation; it's just a knowing of what's being said. She says, "*Imagine if people were to focus on communication as an evolutionary process of over 10,000 years—this is how it would go.*"

One might be able to fathom how this "instantaneous" knowing could be akin to a thought-bubble; this is how it has been described to us in the Ghost Society. A thought is far more expansive than words; words are simply representative, while the thought can be quite multidimensional—sending images, sounds, and emotions, which words can only *describe*. Moreover, these communicative thoughts would require no verbiage, therefore language would not be a barrier between people—allowing others to finally communicate who had earlier been prohibited by the nature of geography and culture, as described by Sarah's grandfather from the Middle East:

He says, "*Oh boy, when you realize there is no language barrier, it really opens things up in terms of group dynamics in understanding other people.*'" He's making me feel like, here on earth, because of the different languages, relations are more confounding and confusing than what they need to be...because we're struggling with how the words are being interpreted in terms of meaning. Whereas over there, since they don't use language, and it's just some kind of knowing... there is a coming together and a joining of every...race and nationality, "*because we have perfect understanding of what the other person is intending to say.*"

At last, it seems on the Other Side that communication no longer keeps humanity splintered, but that everyone can come together without confusion and can contribute more in the process of dialogue than what we could here on earth.

Other things, such as dancing and making love, also continue on the Other Side. According to Nancy's father, the afterlife has its own version of dancing clubs! He described it thusly:

> He says, "Yeah, there's lots of clubs around here for things like dancing and stuff...You can still do that stuff." Dancing...He immediately drew clubs out here...Here, here, here, for all different kinds of things.

From Marti's mother in session ten:

> Movement is definitely there...And music...Music... She also had music abilities...She puts it on herself. She contributes to the group.

Gabi's mother from session thirteen apparently enjoyed dancing while she was on earth. However, certain attributes from the Other Side had compelled her to give it up and go do something different—running!

> There's something about the feet...Are you dancing? She makes me feel negative, as if "I don't. I could, but I'm choosing not to." She's like, you can dance, you can dance...She is enjoying running. I keep seeing running. She's saying, "It makes me feel alive. It gets things going, gets things going." When she runs, she can feel the connections to things. It's meditative, I would say.

Since the nature of the environment is different from earth, a few spirits were kind enough to not only mention they could do more than simply dance, they were able to do things we currently can't do thanks to earth's gravity! Here's what Debbie's father had to say from session seven:

> He's making me feel like, "The physical movement—we can do it a whole lot freer than what we do on earth because...the earth body has so much weight because of gravity, that movement is

limited in comparison to what we can do here." And they still do physical-like activities.

From M.G.'s mother in session eight:

> She says, *"Yes, yes, yes, we can do all of these things and more."* She shows me flying up off the ground, so they don't have gravity there or something. There's this movement that is more fluid and freeing...

As for making love, apparently that joy isn't restricted simply to earth, as reported by these happy spirits. Cynthia's father in session five:

> He's making me feel like...the making love thing, definitely. He must have been a ladies man.

Cynthia laughed with an emphatic "Yes." Her father continued:

> He's making me feel like, the making love thing is here... *"and I have not been abstaining."*

For Sarah's Muslim grandfather, he started out by explaining his thoughts on the sexual act while he was alive on earth, then went on to say how he's changed his views somewhat since being on the Other Side:

> When I say making love, he says *"fornicating."* They did not make love for love's purpose over there in the Middle East, did they? It was for just having kids. He makes me feel like this was a very isolated thing on earth for him. When I say *"making love,"* he does not give me the impression of *"this is how I was when I was here; making love for love's purpose."* There was not that freedom with it. He actually thinks that was a good thing. It kept people out of trouble. It's like he's saying, *"To me, people get too wrapped up in the sexual act and it creates too many bad events."* He's like, *"I wasn't too much into that. I've since loosened up a bit, I enjoy it now. But still..."* He's not

this gigolo kind of guy. He gets the enjoyment out of it...He doesn't lust. He doesn't have that.

But as we all know, physical lust does not translate to love and the sharing of deep, personal, spiritual energies. When that convergence of passion occurs on the Other Side, the dynamics of the sexual union take on a much more beautiful expression, apparently to the point that the physical act isn't even required! Somehow, it's the enjoyment and expression of the *energy*. This was brought home by Terri's grandmother, Rose. While Rose was alive on earth, she led quite the passionate life and would definitely have been the one to comment on the nature of sex from the Other Side:

> I've never had this response before. She says regarding the act of making love over there, they seem to be able to outdo it. It has something to do with energetic dynamics from what she's showing me. From here on earth the physical act produces qualities of energy, which is the whole point of why we get into it, from what she's showing me. And she's making me feel like, you could engage in the same physical act over there, but you don't need to. Because the ability to intermingle and create ecstatic urging and rapture type sensations is natural over there—the physical act isn't required to achieve that. She's actually discovered a way to really make love to heights she never knew when she was here. But she's saying, to bring it down to another level like dancing, yes, she shows me the people in the ballrooms still tapping their feet, waltzing, doing that sort of thing. Physical things, physical activities, that sort of thing, she says yes, you can still do that stuff. But we can do so much more beyond that.

Diane put her own humorous spin on the subject. She kept showing me images that I was too embarrassed to speak of with my wife! According to Heidi, Diane was not one to hold back her commentary or refrain from being blunt. Here is Diane's spin:

Wow, things can get really, uh, "creative"…Let's just say you can do physical things, but you can do them in ways over there that you can't do them here. It's like some exotic circus act. She says, *"If you think orgasm is good on earth, wait 'til you have it on the Other Side!"*

In the end, not only is communication completely freed up and understood among all spirits, so too are the abilities of exchanging personal energy, fun, and physical activities—they are apparently quite unmatched when compared to life on earth. Existence, in all its varied aspects, according to the spirits, becomes much more dimensional and expansive on the Other Side, which ultimately provides new insight, clarity, and experiences beyond what we can currently achieve.

14

Are There Different Languages in the Afterlife? What Is Communication Like?

Yes, we did touch on this in the last question. However, the previous question was focused mainly on the overall view of communication and not the specifics. For instance, if telepathy was the main mode of dialogue, would it be similar to speech? Could someone talk telepathically to an English native *and* a Chinese native? Would they be hearing the communication in their own respective tongue? Or would the language of telepathy be hindered by the language of the individual?

As indicated by the spirits from the latter question, language is not an issue when it comes to communication on the Other Side. What this inquiry ultimately revealed was *how* that dialogue was transmitted and received between the two parties. At first, it appears as just a form of "knowing," as revealed by Leah's friend, Michael:

> It's just a knowing. He gives me an image of two people—a Hindu and an American. The intention of the communication leaves one and goes into the other. The information one wants to convey, strikes something within the individual receiving it and is processed as a knowing. It's like language doesn't even exist; it's like an instant knowing of what the other person is trying to convey and is done from within. He's saying, *"That tower of Babel stuff, that language thing, is totally on earth."*

But there were indications that came out through the sittings which suggested it was much more than that. Diving down into the "experience" of the communication processes revealed that the information being transmitted was often received or wrapped up in a "feeling tone" quality.

Before this question came up, Brandon from session two was suddenly replaced by Jodi's ex-husband, who she lovingly calls "Ock." As before, Ock had to supply me with several bits of data to validate he was coming through before proceeding. After that initial round of substantiation, he leapt forward in answering this question:

He says language in the afterlife is nothing like language on earth. He attaches the word *"feel"* to it, as if to say you *"feel"* what the communication is. You process it through feeling. I actually think these are his words—*"it decodes in your mind."*

The spirit of Nancy's father described the feeling as a type of energy vibration:

He's making me feel like, when the communication comes, it's like an instantaneous vibration. It's vibration that comes over your body...*Boom*...It just delivers the message. The vibration fills your perception of knowledge of what it is being communicated.

The more I asked this question, the more interesting the answers became. On my fifth sitting, Cynthia's father on the Other Side described *where* this vibration occurred:

For some reason, he's showing me the whole side of a body... I don't know what that means...Something with a particular side of the body? The language thing is just...The body just knows...the body just knows.

However, though one spirit may perceive the dialogue entering through the energetic matrix of the body (which again we must realize is an energy field projected and/or controlled by the spirit), the spirit of Debbie's father claimed to receive the communication more in the mind:

> For him, it comes through the head area...And he associates a
> feeling with it. He says, *"You know what's there, because it has
> features to it, it has a feeling, an energy, an intensity to it. And
> it clicks a knowing."* He's saying, *"You know when you think to
> yourself, you sometimes don't even have to use words, you just
> have this communication rolling around in your body and you
> know what it is,"* that's the closest way he can describe it. You
> don't even need to have words attached to it, you just know it.

In any case, whether it's through the body or mind, there is some kind
of recognition and a feeling of the energy brought about by the act of communication. All spirits were unanimous in saying that "talking" by the
Other Side was far more grandiose and understood by levels and degrees
we cannot experience through verbal communication on earth. Gabi's
mother described it like this—with a wonderful analogy:

> She says when you get a message from somebody, it comes
> through as a feeling, and almost instantaneously when you
> receive that feeling, you receive the whole detail of what
> they're trying to tell you; you'll get the picture of what they're
> trying to say, you'll get the feeling they're trying to evoke. It's
> kind of like—this is language on steroids. When we talk on
> earth, it's very one-dimensional, but when they talk, it's very
> three-dimensional. There's all this data that comes in. It's far
> more informative and grand, she says.

Terri's grandmother, Rose, went on to explain that language on earth
was akin to a rickety architecture that, to me (in retrospect), felt like it was
barely adequate to support a soul's meaning in active communication:

> She's saying that when it comes to a separate dialect, language,
> words...that it doesn't matter. There's just a knowing. She's
> making me feel, and the way she's showing me...that earthly
> language is pretty cumbersome. She's showing me raggedy

architecture—boards—to try to get across the meaning and a message that when you're outside the body, that when you're on the Other Side, that rickety-ness completely goes away; that you have full understanding of what the other person is trying to convey. It's what *sparks* inside you.

Communication in the afterlife goes beyond simply mere words—it is an explosion of images, feelings, and recognition of intention. One could say that the internal message a person wishes to communicate completely bypasses language altogether. When we wish to talk, we translate our message into code—language—that is then picked up and interpreted by the person we are communicating with. On the Other Side, that middle step of language is eliminated, thereby having less distortion and fuller understanding from spirit to spirit.

Do You Still Have Inner Challenges or Things That Cause Stress?

We have always heard throughout history that heaven was a place of pure joy and felicity. The iconography is, of course, sitting on a cloud and plucking a harp (a bit too boring for me, but may be enjoyable for some). I wanted to know if spirits really led care-free lives. Even if one had no physical body like what one has on earth and the pains that come with it, that doesn't mean there aren't other stressors in one's existence. What about psychological issues? Phobias? Could you still "just not like someone" and have to deal with the rubbish surrounding all that?

I have had several sittings where it was apparent that two people who didn't get along while physically alive didn't necessarily kiss and make up on the Other Side. Sometimes, the history between these individuals is so volatile, that they leave the inequities up to "future" personalities to balance out. Yes, life on the Other Side is filled with an overabundance of love, light, and forgiveness; but that doesn't always happen between people for a variety of reasons.

In the fourteen sessions, all the spirits revealed the same thing: the environment and lifestyle of the spiritual world does not produce stressful *situations* as we have come to know them on earth. I think this has to do in part to the absence of a Time and Space structure. This was hinted at in session thirteen. That, in combination with a newfound perspective on one's self, relegates any stress to the experience of being that personality. In other words, stress on the Other Side is a personal issue related to what a spirit is holding onto within him or herself, existing for the purpose of uncovering or working through the issue. This was the unanimous message from every one of my spiritual guests, especially Gabi's mother:

> She says, *"I have inner challenges, but not things that cause me stress."* She says, *"Part of the things in life that you carry over are your inner things you are working on."* She says, *"Once you realize you don't die, that takes the teeth out of it; it takes the bite out of all the stress about the thoughts of your challenges."* She says, *"On earth, you guys really beat yourself up about your inner challenges—like, 'This is going to kill me if I don't figure this out.' But then you realize you cannot die, so you approach your inner challenges from a much more loving and caring perspective. Instead of beating yourself up, you go, 'Okay, everything is going to be all right; I will figure it out. I have TIME to figure it out.' At that point, you're much more nurturing and loving to yourself."* She says, *"You just know in your heart that you will make it."*

So when you have all eternity to better yourself, you obviously don't stress out from the sense of any clock ticking. I like that. Time really does "lose its teeth" on the Other Side. And that alone must surely make everyone blissful. This was also mentioned by Terri K.'s brother from my ninth sitting:

> When you say inner challenges, he says *"yes"* to that. But stress, no. *"I wouldn't call it stressful."* He's saying it's not stressful because you are relieved of a timetable. You are relieved from having to answer to something other than yourself. It's like you're not put under this microscope anymore.

Gabi's mom also went on to say how we can see the freedom of eternity in working out our issues by observing children. This was an important message, as Gabi has a child of her own with whom she could relate her mom's message:

She says you are in the prime opportunity to see it, you will see it in the little kids. They have that in their energy; you can see it—that they know they'll make it. They are always testing the boundaries, and they have no fear in testing those limits. That is because they haven't let go of what they came in knowing; that is, *"I have all the time in the world."* For your son, she says when it comes to his inner challenges that he will have in his life, that's the stuff he needs to be nurtured on and cared for. But for the other stuff from which he can be physically harmed... You need to discipline him...still on earth, there are still things that can happen to him, that can leave an impact and can be harmful. *"If what he's going to go through is going to be damaging...put a foot down."*

Like questions before this, the answers from spirit were quite undisputed that the Other Side did not produce stressful situations in the way we have them on earth. This didn't mean life was completely stress-free, but the stresses one felt were self-induced, as told by Jodi's ex-husband in my second session:

He says you bring inner challenges and stress over here from within you, but in terms of this place giving you inner challenges and stresses, no. Not here. He says, *"You own it. You own the inner challenges, you own the inner stresses. It's nothing over here."*

Certain emotions and hang-ups can still bring inner stress and challenges, as evidenced by Nancy's father. He was mentioning a relationship with his brother, first by showing me my symbolic image for "sibling," and then telling me there was a huge gap in both age and personality between the two of them. Nancy confirmed my impressions and her father unloaded the following:

When it comes to feeling regret, he says *"brother."* When it comes to regrets, there are a lot with his brother.

So it's apparent that we can still carry stress and challenges about other people—even if they are on the Other Side with us.

Diane from session fourteen alluded that stress on the Other Side is often attributed to the tendencies of the person feeling it. What this suggests to me is, if you are a worrywart on earth, you might still carry some of that preoccupation in the afterlife, based on what Diane had to say:

> She says there are some people who hold themselves very seriously in their development and journey…that they will take themselves too seriously…And in being that serious will develop an inner stress, which could be interpreted as an inner challenge. Aside from that, she says nobody is forcing you to do anything, nobody is telling you to do anything. *"There isn't a boss chewing on your ass."* It's all very much self-directed. She writes the word *"self"* out in front of me. *"Self-motived and self-directed."* It's going to depend on the character of the individual as to inner challenges, stress, and issues. She says, *"Yes, I have things that I'm working on, but I try not to let it get to a point where it brings my energy down or makes me concerned."* She says, *"I learned a lot from the Life Review, in terms of holding stress in the body."*

As for other stresses which could be conditioned by life on the Other Side, Nancy's father from session three had this to say:

> He says, *"Not stress like you guys have; your stress is totally different from our stress."* Stress isn't the word he would attach to what he's got going on. For him, he's got this realization that *"I have lessons to learn,"* and it's that *"not having learned them yet"* which creates what we put the term *"stress"* on. But he says it's not really stressful, you just have this knowing that you don't have a certain knowledge that you need to get…That's your *"discordance."*

Kourtnie's father from session twelve also gave his opinion on why he thought stress existed on earth in comparison to the Other Side. It appears we've lost our sense of community, or at least our awareness to that which we are all a part of—the wonderment of the universe:

> He says, *"We always have some kind of stress in our lives; that's the point of living—to have some stress and overcome it."* But he's like, *"No, no, no, it's not like earth."* He says, *"While you are on earth, you are blind to what you are capable of, what your potentials are...You are kind of blind to those things about yourself and so you are blind to what's there for you."* He makes me feel like, over there on the Other Side, there's this unity, expression, that is never without..."*You are always being reminded and are aware of your possibilities. You don't feel like you've been left alone in the dark, which is how you feel on earth. You just have this awareness."*

So if a spirit could feel stress, what were they stressing over? Out of the fourteen sittings conducted for this experiment, there really were only two sources for unease. The first was quite logical to my mind: looking back to those of us on earth and seeing what we were up to. The second was owning their own need or desire for development and working through their own attachments.

Our family members on the Other Side care a lot about us, so when we are in painful situations here, they are aware of it. The loss of a job, a divorce, a medical crisis—these are all things which bring stress to any compassionate observer, especially if that observer is a loving, close relative now living in the afterlife. If you were a spirit and saw your son or daughter on earth in emotional, psychological, or certainly physical pain, you would no doubt be spurred by the crisis to do what you could to help. From Grace's grandmother in session four:

> She's saying there are people on the Other Side that don't have inner challenges and stress like you and I have, but they sometimes stress over people they are watching back here on earth...because you get concerned for people you've left behind, family members...She's doing this whole family ties thing...Because the family ties are so strong in the Orient..."I

know people here that stress themselves out in regard to what their family on earth is going through."

Grace interjected with the next logical question: "Can you help from the Other Side?" Her grandmother responded:

"All we can do is ask for more guidance to be given, more energy to be given, but the people down on earth are the ones who make the choice for their own lives."

From Cynthia's father in session five:

I don't know if he joked a lot, but he says, *"If I'm stressed, it's only because I'm looking at you."*

A person's capacity for empathy continues after death. The stress we have in our lives can be observed and shared by our loved ones in spirit. But once spirit turns away from watching, they still acknowledge their own issues.

The greatest form of stress recognized by spirits was owning their own process of development and working through their own perceived needs and desires, as Diane from session fourteen alluded to earlier. Personal evolution apparently doesn't end when we shed our mortal bodies. We each have things we wish to overcome or develop into greater awareness, and it is this inner work, which can sometimes bring stress. This is not unusual. We do this all the time, even while we're alive. I stress at wanting to be more patient and more articulate. Some people stress at how to better interact with a friend or neighbor. For others, they might stress at why they are so shy, or why they are so disruptive. Everybody has things they are working on to improve themselves as a person, and these generate the core of inner challenges—stress—for the developing spirit. From Marti's mother in session ten:

She's making me feel like...The only thing that's stressful is when you start examining your inner self and where you want to go next. She's making me feel like, she's actually at peace with herself and who she is as a being…but she says there's always this compulsion to be better and be greater and be more *full*. It's like a puzzle you keep working out, and this is the drive, I guess. Sometimes…it's not stress like you and I have stress, but it's this puzzle that can confound you, is the sense that I'm getting. It's like, you have so many options in front of you, so many places you can go and things to do, how do you choose which one? And then she asks, *"How do you know if you're choosing the right one?"* She says, *"Don't make it feel like the stress you have on earth, because it's really not that way."* It's one of those internal things; when you're at a crossroads and you're kind of making decisions, and you wonder if this is going to produce a better outcome overall. Sometimes you never know.

Then Marti asked the question: "Does it even matter?" This is how the reply came:

> For her, yes. For her, it feels like it does matter. For her, she has personal integrity that she wants to keep intact. *"Cautious"* isn't the right word, but she wants to be very perceptive in looking at what she's doing before she goes through with it.

From M.G.'s mother in session eight:

> Stress…No, there's no real sense of stress. Inner challenges… it's only what she would perceive as growth in the individual for the entire entity. Stress like what we have—pressures on us and the demands of things—no, no, no, definitely not like that at all. *"The stress comes in engaging your own consciousness for development,"* she's making me feel.

So even though we have traditionally been taught that the afterlife, or "heaven," is stress-free, it might really depend on one's own disposition. I think it's safe to say that heaven will not put any undo stress upon you—there will not be any demands which induce a stressful or fearful situation. This does not mean that in your own personality you won't create your own stress for your own purposes. As we'll find out later in the Interviews, the love fully expressed in the afterlife in conjunction with the endless avenues for learning will make our ideas of stress on earth toxic and destructive in comparison to what freedoms we have on the Other Side, even when we're stressed.

How Do You Perceive Yourself in The Flow of Time? Does Time Have Any Meaning?

This question was inspired by my work in ghost research, as I ask it on every investigation I attend. It is also the question that I have received an answer to over and over again with a consistent response: *"No, not affected by Time."*

I have always wondered what it must be like for a spirit. Are they at the center of a wheel—the hub—and all Time passes around them? If they are not affected by Time, then current theories being postulated in physics—which state that the past, present, and future are all happening simultaneously—must be correct. This leaves one baffled, as it is difficult to understand how experiences would be measured or remembered by a soul in the afterlife if the events were not "separated out" on a timeline. Naturally, this question always left me salivating for the answers during the sessions.

As it turns out, Time appears to be a matter of consciousness. That is, we choose to filter our experiences in a timeline fashion; however, there isn't a "law" of Time measurement, e.g., sixty seconds equals one minute, everywhere in the universe. As Albert Einstein and other scientists have shown, Time is relative and exists in rhythms. We know this by how we respond to our own experiences—"Today just dragged by," or, "It was over before I knew it." It's all perceptual then—and even more so on the Other Side. This is how Michael from my first session responded to this question:

He still perceives some kind of movement of Time, but says it's not what we would perceive as Time. He is aware of the simultaneous nature, but is unwilling to spread himself out along that yet, is what he's showing me. He's giving me the past, present, and future, and then he's here and working in his own sort of moment-by-moment experience. He says it's different for him, and *"I'm not willing to spread myself out into this yet."*

Cynthia's father in session five had this to say:

He says this is one of the really unique quirks to this environment, the No-Time quirk. Then he backs up and says, *"I can view my day-to-day experience in this linear type fashion."* So he does view his life in a this-first-this-second-this-third expression, but then says none of it really matters that way. He collapses it and makes it like an accordion. This is really what Time is and we just stretch it out. He says, *"Our Time here on the Other Side is completely not relevant to your Time there. This is where the worlds disconnect."* It's like he pulls a second earth out and disconnects it and says this is where we really separate in terms of our atmosphere and environment. *"Time doesn't have meaning here, where you guys really drag things out."*

From Sarah's grandfather in session six:

He says that over there, Time has no meaning. It's completely open, it's completely free. *"Time is a process that whittles down products of experience."* He says, *"Now we can consciously put ourselves in a moment-by-moment experience, but we accept it as an illusion."*

Yes, the process of Time can get quite baffling—and has been that way for me on several occasions. The more I listened, the more I kept hearing from the spirits that they don't perceive Time as we do, but yet still measured their experiences in some type of linear fashion, if only to experience the full breadth of their actions. This is what M.G.'s mother from session eight brought forward, helping to give a glimpse of how spirits think of Time:

> She says Time is only there as a structure for engaging events. She backs up here, makes me feel like, "*I understand Time is an illusion, it's not real. On the other hand, I create within the bounds of Time in order to witness…to view the experiences.*"

From this response, one could almost imagine Time as being like a canvas that an artist paints his or her life upon. Time needs to be there in order to view the color, the strokes, the multidimensionality of the impressions. Diane from session fourteen expressed Time through comparison:

> She says Time for us on earth is very dragged out. When she says that, she takes Time and stretches it like a rubber band. So for her, Time is…She says, "*I have my own view of Time and it's different from yours. Where you see Time as linear, I see Time as circular.*" She folds it up…Pulls it out and says, "*I see it as circular.*" She says she still perceives herself moment-by-moment, but can't do it linearly. She says, "*I am eternal, I am eternal…*" She says to view it like a funnel.

From Kourtnie's father in session twelve:

> He says, "*I don't see myself in the flow of Time as you see Time,*" but he does make me feel like he still measures his experiences through a Time-like field of nature, but that's his choice. On some level, he knows that's BS, but he still likes to quantify things, so he has to have things broken down for him. In a No-Time zone, he's making me feel like there's this sense of not having control to do that. So he still breaks things down in a this-first-that-second manner, to quantify things; but he says it's different than what's experienced on earth.

I'm not sure what Kourtnie's father meant when he said there wasn't a sense of having control in a No-Time zone. That may have just been his opinion of what it feels like to work in an environment that appears to not have any boundaries; it gets hard to quantify and measure without some type of distinction.

In a few instances, the spirits gave me a clue as to what existence from a No-Time perspective was like. In those moments, the notion of separation between earth and spirit was wiped away, as the departed mentioned being in the presence of the sitter as he or she existed on the Other Side! That is, at some point in Time, we will all die and will be on the Other Side. Well, apparently for those spirits who have this wisdom of No-Time, they can be in the presence of the sitter's future self. From Jodi's ex-husband, Ock, in session two:

> He shows Time like an ocean that has different currents going along at the same time (no pun intended). Like an upper current, a middle current, and a lower current. In some ways, you're already there because of the way Time operates. He says he's already enjoying you there. But that's a very hard thing to grasp; it's a very hard concept to grasp. He shows me upper, middle, and lower. This complete lower one, he says is this idea of simultaneous time…Here, it's all wrapped up…"*In that state, I can feel you and me wrapped up. It's very real…*" It's very—another one of his words—"*cogent.*" He says, "*In order for me to reach that state, I have to go into that middle ground… It's almost like a meditative state.*"

From Debbie's father in session seven:

> He says this is one of the things that really magnetized him to go forward into the spirit world. He seemed to have some kind of recollection or knowledge that Time was not a factor… and therefore when he reached wherever he was going, you, Debbie, were already there—because without Time, part of you would already be there. So, it was like, "*I was already reunited with my family…*" Now, he says, "*This is not something you're going to easily grasp, but you're already there. You're there.*"

It's quite difficult to grasp the nature of experience without perceiving it in some kind of linear fashion. It was still my impression that even though the spirits acknowledged the existence of No-Time, they themselves still chose on some level to filter their own experiences in a way similar to how they had on earth. Whether this impression is due to the limitations of this world or my own mind, I cannot say. The best analogy I have is of viewing the earth from space. On earth we have over forty different time zones. In the continental United States, we have Eastern, Central, Mountain, and Pacific Time Zones – but the fact of the matter is, these times are occurring simultaneously. It doesn't matter that these and all the other zones exist, for they are merely an illusion from the point-of-view of an astronaut out in space who would see them all occurring at once. Somehow, this is how Time must be from the angle of spirit.

In the land of spirits, my feeling is that they continue to work in a "Time-like" field as well. Maybe because they still don't completely understand it either. From Ock in session two:

> He says the consciousness…The act of being…"*You filter Time.*" He says in some respects he still lives a moment-by-moment experience, but he understands that he unfolds it, that he's attached to the unfolding. He understands that deep down, the reality of things is simultaneous. It's some kind of conscious understanding or will of understanding that has to be achieved before you can be in this spot all the time. It's almost like, "*I know about this, but I don't know it, so I can't be there all the time, but I am aware that this is probably the reality of things…But this is where I'm at.*"

From Sarah's grandfather in session six:

> He's making me feel like, in some ways, "*We understand there is no such thing as Time, but there are certain components to that knowledge we don't quite grasp, so we don't necessarily view everything as this one big jumbled up composite. That's a knowledge thing; that's a gained wisdom perspective. Right now, it's a surface-knowledge thing.*" He says, "*This is something*

we'll get into later, as we develop, as we grow and mature into the spiritual beings that we are. This will come into perspective later."

For others, they had accepted the notion of No-Time and learned somehow to live within it. What I found interesting was how they equated the physical world with Time—and in the process of communicating back to earth, whether it be communication through a medium or simply visiting as an apparition, smell, or a feeling to their loved one here, they expressed having to re-enter a Time field, as if it were a function of design in earthly life; a part of its architecture. From Terri's grandmother, Rose:

She shows Time to me like a bowl—that inside the contents of this bowl is No-Time. But in order for you to communicate here on earth with what we're doing right now as mediumship, she has to somehow enter the field of consciousness of Time. She's showing it to me like diving into a pool of water. You know when you dive into a pool of water and everything slows down, that's what she's showing to me. She's saying, *"Over here where we're at, everything is free flowing, quick, and Time doesn't matter. But in order to do this sort of thing here, slowing down, it's like jumping into water, in order to coordinate."* At that point Time takes on a certain relevance. But that only has to do with the nature of your experience. She's saying, *"You walk through Time and this is just part of how things were designed. When you're on earth, you walk through Time. When you get over here, you don't."*

From Teri K.'s brother in session nine:

He's pulling me completely out and says, *"I have nothing to do with Time."* He says, *"The only thing I have to deal with, with Time, is doing this with you and then I'm back out."* In saying that, he's referencing that it's a mental thing...that Time is a mental construct that you can focus into and work within.

As we can see, just because spirits reveal they are not living in Time, they admit they don't know all the nuances. Plus, it must be even harder to try and explain to those of us back here in the physical Time-oriented reality how the ultimate reality of No-Time really works. However, as we will see from diving deeper into the Interviews, though it is difficult to grasp the field of No-Time psychologically, there are some highly fascinating factors that come into view when the barrier of Time is released from perceptual reality.

17

If You Perceive Time, Do You See Any Past Lives You Have Had? How Would You Describe That? What About the Akashic Record? Can You Converse With a Previous "You"?

Here I must somewhat step out of the discussion to talk a little about physics in relation to Time. Modern physicists—particularly those who work in quantum mechanics—acknowledge that Time is all relative to the observer. As stated in the last chapter, sixty seconds doesn't always equal one minute. There have been some excellent thought-experiments, which demonstrate this, most notably the twins who remain separated in a space-flight scenario. The way this story goes, one twin, we'll call him "Joe," leaves earth on a rocket ship traveling near the speed of light and returns several years later to see his twin brother, "John." Due to time dilation revealed in the special theory of relativity, Joe will actually return younger than his twin brother, who has aged significantly at earth's rate.

Moreover, scientific studies have demonstrated the ability of the present to go backward and affect the past. Replicated tests using random number generators, recorded audio, and in some cases, recorded video, have revealed that with enough mental intention, a goal can be seeded in the present moment, yet also reach backward to affect the past. One of the most fun examples of this functionality is that psycho-spiritual event most people call "Divine Parking." Think about it. You're always two minutes away from the parking lot when you throw out the intention for "that perfect parking spot." Yet for the spot to actually become available, you would have to factor in the time spent at stoplights, detours, and any pedestrians in your way. Additionally, it must be coordinated with the person who may currently be occupying the spot you receive—how that person needs to get through the store check-out line, pack the groceries into the car, then pull out and leave the spot vacant just long enough so somebody else doesn't come along and steal it before you arrive! It is an amazing orchestration that requires mathematical precision with regard to Time—and some people are absolute masters of it. My wife and I have a friend who lives in a highly populated metropolitan area, but all she has to do is "ask Ramone!" just a few blocks from where she wants to park. Lo and behold, her "parking angel" Ramone always comes through. Seriously. We've been with her on several occasions to see it happen. When you stop to consider this incredible ability, it dawns on you that the "simple" act of requesting Divine Parking two minutes from the parking lot may actually have reached backward in Time to inform you when to have left the house!

So when we begin to factor in what scientists have been studying (and have most likely known since the 1960s, if not longer), the past, present, and future are all "wrapped up" in a sort of simultaneous song of Being.

If this were the case—that all Time is happening simultaneously if we discard the Time filter—then such things as past lives would become apparent to a modern-day spirit traveler. Without the barriers of Time to "pull things apart," that which was the past would be concurrent with the present as well as the future. Reincarnation at that point loses its standard "this-life-before-that" meaning and equates more with the idea of simultaneous selves, rather than reincarnational selves. This would explain why a medium could communicate with a soul from the 1500s while simultaneously another person could perceive that ancient lifetime as being a "past life" they once lived. It's not that the soul from the 1500s no longer exists in the spirit world because it has descended back to earth, but instead—because all Time is wrapped up and simultaneous—that a soul from the 1500s is still an independent personality existing in the spirit world. This doesn't negate the possibility that there could be another personality here in the modern era who springs from the same source material (Oversoul) which is psychically and spiritually bound to the events experienced by the other personality. This is akin to the identical twin phenomenon most people are familiar with, where a zygote from one fertilized egg separates and forms two embryos, each reflecting the same genetic material. And we can carry the twin analogy further, where there have been identical twins who—even after being separated at birth—have ended up marrying spouses with the same first name, getting the same kind of dog, and miraculously working in similar fields and even breaking the same bones! This is not too different from the concept of an Oversoul existing throughout Time with simultaneous selves.

So imagine what it must be like to lose the trapping of Time when moving into the spirit world and discover these other "You's" that have existed (and will exist) throughout history.

This particular question received some of the best EVPs (electronic voice phenomena) from the entire series, as the spirits thought the question quite exciting and out-of-the-box. Indeed, their responses clearly indicated a willingness to educate my sitters and me in regard to reincarnation and simultaneous personalities—and how the spirits acknowledged their connections to these previous selves. Let's start with the spirit of Michael, from session one:

> He's saying, "*Yes, I see past personalities*," but for some reason, he separates himself from them, as if to say there is a membrane or something there that keeps them separated somehow. Yet, in some strange way, they are aware of one another. He's showing me...a past personality looking up at him and recognizing the connection. I get the feeling he's not connecting with these past ones because they are part of his issues. It's more of an emotional thing that he says, "*I don't want to go back here. I don't want to connect with these...It's not that I can't, but I'm keeping the membrane here for a reason.*"

From Nancy's father in session three:

> Actually he does make me feel like he does perceive past lives...other persons he had been, or his soul had been. He recognizes them, but he does not socialize with them. It's not because he's afraid, it's just because he doesn't want to get caught up in the whole Time thing. He understands he is his

own individual and these are just aspects of a greater portion of his being, but he still wants to move forward in expressing himself, who he is as an individual, and not let any of these others dictate to him...or "codify" his possibilities.

From Grace's grandmother in session four:

> She says, "*I can look behind me and see past lives.*" She says, "*Well, when there is No-Time, then these people who you perceive you were are also there.*" However, she...she does this to say, "*I don't associate with them. I know of them, they are a part me in here, we are connected in that way...I am also aware I am somewhat individual from these people, yet we are connected.*"

As we can see from the responses, we can come into the world of Time and Space with issues and lessons the greater portion of our Self (the Oversoul) is working to understand and balance out. These issues, it seems, can stem from the past (as well as future) personalities that we are connected to.

This may sound a bit confusing. Let's take the analogy of a hand to demonstrate this phenomenon. You could say the five fingers of your hand represent five different lifetimes, yet they all belong to the same hand. However, in the field of Time, only one finger is perceived as being present, with each other finger existing separately in a different era. But because they are the same hand, they are working through many of the same issues and lessons from one era to another, and on occasion would identify him or herself as being an extension of another finger—for indeed they are that (an extension), but still uniquely a personality all their own, birthed from the same source as an expression of that greater entity—the whole hand (Oversoul).

Diane from session fourteen likened the concept to that of holography. In holography, you can take a snapshot of a three-dimensional object using laser light, mirrors, and a photographic plate. What happens is that an image of the object gets transferred onto the plate in an interference pattern, which when a light is reflected off of or shown through the plate, recreates the image in three dimensions. What's more, if the plate were to

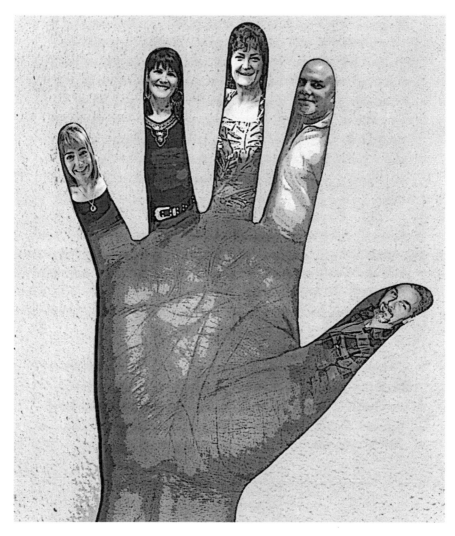

be broken into little pieces, each piece would still show the full image of the original object in 3-D when hit with light. The analogy here is, each individual reincarnational self is a part of a holographic whole, where each self contains the imprint of the whole Oversoul. Diane's description of it is excellent, as would be expected from a scientist:

> She says when it comes to reincarnational selves..."*These are the prisms of the Oversoul in the linear environment.*" It's the holographic model thing. She says, since it's the holographic

model…"*Take one of those little pieces of the hologram…It can also reflect upon its own little piece in conjunction with the larger image it is a part of.*" She says that will give an understanding of the personality of the individual. She says it has to do with expression and free will, even though it is a hologram of the big picture. She says, "*Over here, with No-Time, it's all still spread out.*" And she is like, "*Yes, you can definitely converse with a previous you, especially if you're a hologram…*" She's also showing it to me as pancake layers, stacked on top of each other.

For some in the spirit world, because we don't normally think in simultaneous terms, a soul could look at these other personalities and see them with emotional upset. Especially if issues that were energetically filtered through the simultaneous personalities, to grapple with while incarnated on earth, had been the drama of one's life. This appeared to be the case with several spirits I talked with:

He says for some people it is very difficult to deal with these other portions of themselves, because of what these lives ex-perienced…"*There's still all this emotion, there's still attachment to these things to what these other 'You's' went through…There's fear that gets attached…You get too caught up in yourself.*"

Michael from session one went on to describe it like this:

He says a lot of people have this perspective of the present being impacted from the past…so they don't want to go back there and focus on past lives. They still associate this with, even though it is a separate and individual entity so to speak, the connections that exist…People don't want to go back and relive what they think as the past…even though they see this previous personality kind of going off on its own…because it was so emotional and everything…It was a life that they un-derstand they are connected to in some way, and they don't necessarily go back to either integrate or socialize with the past personality. He says some do, some understand there's a greater thing going on here and they're willing to do that. Other people are just too afraid."

From Kourtnie's father in session twelve:

> He says he's aware of what we would call past personalities and past lives...And he's met a few of them. But he...he didn't like them because they reminded him too much of his youth. Some of that behavior was carried over from these other personalities. He says in meeting these others, he wanted to blame them for how he was, even though they were all kind of one and the same anyway.

From Nancy's father in session three:

> I think he was curious about who all these other people he used to be were, or who he was associated to. Then I think he went to see one or two of them, but never approached them...It's like, "I saw them, and certain things came back to mind or consciousness, and I just backed off."

The more the spirits revealed about the simultaneous personalities and connections to them, the more they explained about the need for the Akashic Record. The Akashic Record is the name given to the compendium of cosmic knowledge encoded in the non-physical plane of existence containing all the history and recorded thoughts of humanity—like a library in the "Mind of God." One could also think of it as a dimension of consciousness that contains a vibrational record of every soul and its journey. The concept goes back to Vedic times (and the name derives from the Sanskrit for "sky," "space," or "ether") but was popularized by the Theosophists in the nineteenth century. As it turns out, the existence of this "library" is validated by the spirits, and they tell how it is quite necessary when it comes to dealing with simultaneous/reincarnational personalities. As described by the spirits, the Akashic Record allows for a small degree of separation when looking at the interconnected soul of a past or future life. Here's how Jodi's ex-husband, Ock, in session two described it:

> Akashic Record…He says it's written on the wind. *"All of your life is written on the wind, in space…"* Something like that…It's just recorded everywhere is the sense that he's giving me. *"The Book of Life thing is the closest reference you can get, but it's not a book, per se.'"* Although he corrects me and says, *"A lot of people will manifest or create a book they can look in…"* He says some people don't like this idea of meeting their other selves, so they'd much rather read about it, because it could become too personal or too emotional to actually go meet another lifetime of themselves. But he says it's such a cool thing; you should do it.

From Nancy's father in session three:

> He's showing me the bookshelf with the book you pull off where you supposedly read about your past lives…He says it's easier to do that, because it's written down, you can sort of dissociate yourself from it…It's like you're a degree separate…He did spend some time doing that, when he first got over there.

From Grace's grandmother in session four:

> She says, *"This is the easiest way for people like me to confirm these other identities and to understand them."* In our terminology, it's the Life Book…She's saying this is the easiest way to answer these questions for yourself without getting emotionally involved…You are somewhat detached. *"When you are looking into your own face from a past life, it can get …"* There's a lot of emotion going on, a lot of attachment…things that really work you up inside. It's much easier to do it with detachment when looking at a book. She says, *"You've got to understand the past lives are still going on…We are still individuals, yet we*

come from the same mold. And our paths and our virtual lives are patterned after one another…These patterns grow, change, but they will always have certain things that are likened to one another, so you can see yourself in these lives and say 'this was me' yet at the same time, they are their own person. You don't lose your identity…" She's saying when you, Grace, when you die, you will still be Grace, but there's going to be another person back here, that could be named Evelyn, that the two of you come from the same energy, so you could say you are this person, yet you are still Grace and this is Evelyn. And there will be many similarities between the two, since you are cast from the same mold.

Sarah's grandfather from session six added this:

He's showing me a big building…This is the library…Is this literal or figurative? He's making me feel it's more figurative, but says it can be whatever you want it to be. He says, *"If you want to open up a book about your lives, there's a book about you there. You can read about your histories and lives from a book."* He's making me feel like, *"Many people prefer to do it this way because it otherwise gets very emotional; there are dynamics in being able to speak to yourself that you down on earth are really quite unaware of…So many people prefer to leave these other identities alone and would rather read about them in a book in order to have a certain level of detachment…"* He's making me feel like he had a very close connection to a previous life which was way, way, way back…and he spent considerable time researching that one. He may actually have talked to that identity. But any recent, up front ones, he glossed right over.

Debbie's father from session seven had this to say:

He says the Akashic Record is the low-down way of reviewing these lifetimes. *"You don't have to deal with the people directly, you don't have to get all caught up in the emotional end of it;*

it's a form of separation—it's a psychological thing." So the book will lay out things that happened in…points in lifetimes, meanings in lifetimes, relationships in lifetimes. He says a lot of people have a lot of fun seeing where the relationships have carried on, but they don't like to necessarily get caught up in the emotional end of it. They prefer it rather "dry."

And Kourntie's father in session twelve:

He likes the Akashic Record…I'm glued to it. He says he's aware of what we would call past personalities and past lives… He's saying, *"I distanced myself from them and I decided to use the Akashic Record to learn more about who they were and who I am."* He says they put you in this book that you can gain access to…And you don't have to deal with the crap that's back here. I think being in the actual presence of these other selves brings up this whole realm of stuff that becomes very emotional and very personal…That's when he backed away and tried this other route.

Diane from session fourteen gave me her view of the Akashic Record in her typical, left-brained, scientific way:

She says, *"Honey, the Akashic Record is a metaphor for the lives that are 'written in the universe.'"* She's showing me this field of space and saying, *"Take two or three lives here, their experiences are more or less laid out like data…There's no emotion attached to it. You can access the data if you want to…Everything is written in the universe and accessible…"* She acknowledges that…When you get into the "lower" life forms or intellects, the spirit world requires it to be accessible to their level of awareness; let's face it, some people are less aware than others. So when you hear the stories of it being a library, she says this is adequate. Some people need that reference. Ultimately, it's everywhere, but some people need it to be in that reference.

If you have ever stopped to think about your own internal dialogue going on within your own head—all the judgments and criticisms you shower upon yourself—imagine what it must be like encountering what you could consider other "You's" in personality and form…Where the decisions and actions of these other personalities can have an effect upon you (just as yours would have on them). I can kind of understand why some people would want to avoid talking to another objective portion of themselves. However, this doesn't mean that it *isn't* possible, as I discovered some souls did in fact meet up with a few of these other personalities. Sometimes this union was tough, for the reasons stated above. For others, it opened doors to a better understanding of who they were and why they struggled in certain areas or conversely excelled in others. When approached from this open-possibilities concept, the spirits revealed that the bond between simultaneous selves was quite strong for them—that it was deeper than our perception of family. Ock from session two admitted he had met some of his previous selves:

> He says, *"Yeah, I've met a few of my other selves, and you can converse with them."* He says, *"You want to know what family feels like, you go talk to yourself in these other existences you've had. That will give you a sense of a true family because you can't lie to yourself."* He's got a very healthy ego. He likes his other selves. He likes conversing with them. In some ways, he's able to separate them out as different people, even though he knows they're not. He can see the synchronicities or the similarities between all his other selves, and he likes them.

From Cynthia's father in session five:

> He says, *"Yes, I do see my previous lives"* and he has communicated with some of them. He's laughing and says, *"You'd better have a sense of humor about yourself."* He says it's the only way to deal with the magnitude of realizing this connection with these other "You's" that have existed in history. He says, *"When you can accept your simultaneous 'You's' that have existed in history, this will give you a sense of family like you will not believe."*

But, your father was not a person who enjoyed real egotistical people; he did not like conceit, that's why he did the
"we're not buddy-buddy." Because, part of the reason he feels at
that point, *"If I were to be buddy-buddy with my previous selves,
I would become conceited and egotistical, because I would become too sure of myself."* And that's why he's saying you've got
to have some humor with yourself, so you don't get into that
expression.

And Gabi's mother from session thirteen:

She says she has conversed with previous selves...And she
puts them on the level of sisters...I don't feel like she had a
sister here...For her this is the closest analogy she has...It's
three other selves, all female. There's a couple of her male
energy counterparts that she doesn't want to deal with. She
says, *"I've got selves going all the way through time, but I really
have three or four that I consider sisters...We get together often
to talk about the nature of progression, the nature of life, to talk
about how we can affect or influence the future selves"* that she
is. They all understand on some level their unity and common-
ality with the higher Oversoul. They also acknowledge their
distinctiveness and uniqueness; their individual personalities,
and yet their connection.

Even though Time is perceived to be wrapped up, spirits still acknowledge a type of progression by virtue of simultaneous "future" selves. This
is absolutely baffling to me, as it starts to ask that deep philosophical question: is everything just fate and do we not have free will? According to
spirits in the afterlife, we still have free will, though it is difficult to ex-
press how our choices are placed in a No-Time perspective that we here
on earth would understand. Nevertheless, simultaneous selves are aware
of potential "future" selves that have "future timeline lives" on earth, and
due to the nature of energetic karma, phobias, and the like, are distributed
across the Oversoul; "past personalities" can work toward balancing out
issues in an effort to assist that "future" portion of him or herself. From

M.G.'s mother in session eight:

> She's making me feel like there are past personalities that are
> part of the group she is hanging around with…I keep seeing
> the word "homogeny"…so they've got to be really working
> together. So there is this "*We can communicate with previous
> 'You's'*…" And she's making me feel like, "*The reason we're
> doing this, is because we are still looking at things from this
> future perspective (even though in some ways we know that is an
> illusion)…So in coming together like this, we can get a broader
> and greater 'advance' to the future us and future personalities.*"
> It's like they're taking the ideas and stuff about what needs to
> be worked on and what needs to be developed, and they're
> focusing it on these future personalities that exist at the same
> time on a certain level.

From session eleven, Terri's grandmother, Rose, talked about meeting up
with a future portion of herself on the Other Side:

> She's talking about another portion of herself that we would
> consider reincarnational, but it's two lifetimes into the future.
> She draws two lines and pulls them forward. She says, "*I see
> and I can talk to that consciousness that I would perceive in a
> Time-sense as being another lifetime two lifetimes down the riv-
> er. Over here, that person is here with me; she has individual ex-
> periences and stuff that are unique to her. She has individual and
> unique experiences because of her life on earth. That is what
> separates her from the other personalities. That's what sepa-
> rates the personalities out—It's that they are down in this soup of
> the earthly plain. When they come out of this soup on the Other
> Side, with there being No-Time…They're all connected, but due
> to the nature of separation of experience through the prism of
> Time, each personality retains their individual sense of being.
> However, we understand how this all wraps up into the greater
> identity of 'I.'*"

Rose kept showing me images and impressions that started stacking up, as evidenced from the transcript:

> In looking at this future woman that contains portions of her energy, she says we are all interconnected. *"You can look at your own life and see how your past childhood affects your life as an adult. Same thing here. Even though we may separate ourselves in terms of identity, my experiences and energy have an effect on this future self."* She's using this second level future personality as an inspiration to continue moving forward because she really likes how this lifetime in the future worked out. She's saying *"When you're stuck in the field of Time, it's hard to piece some of this together."* She says it really does make sense when you finally get over there. Then she shows me a brain and says, *"You just bog it all up when you're there on earth. But it is really okay."*

Trying to perceive the nature of consciousness from a No-Time perspective is indeed problematic. Our minds, being a product of Time and Space, may not be able to fully understand how we can have free will and also create karma for other simultaneous selves if no such thing as Time exists. Yet the spirits do acknowledge the other portions of themselves which they have and will be living in the future. For some, they understand the nature of these interconnections and do their best to improve themselves, knowing that such improvements carry a ripple effect throughout the Oversoul and the other personalities. For other spirits, the recognition of these different yet identical people fills them with turbulent emotions, as the connection is still felt as a deeply personal union with a notion of "this is still me."

When does one stop reincarnating? Sarah's Muslim grandfather came through later on in the sittings with an answer to that question which I felt was perfect for this chapter. This is what he had to say:

> *"You don't stop reincarnating until you feel you are ready; until you are done."* He's making me feel like, it's an internal thing, it's a knowing, when you are ready to advance somewhere

else. But then he also says, *"Okay, but keep in mind, Time is an illusion. This idea of you losing who you are right now to become another person is not necessarily really going on. It's another person; you retain who you are and you still live your life in the spiritual realm,"* but this other person—this future person "you," comes from the same—he's showing me, he comes from the same beam of light as you, so carries your…okay… You know how you get some of your qualities as a human from your parents? So you could say your "parents" are in you and you are expressing them in your way. The future self has the experiences, the "DNA" of your experiences. So you are carrying the experiences of your former selves in you like you are carrying your parent's DNA; therefore, yours will also carry forward into the next individual. You're all part of the same energy being, though, that's being parceled out. But the experiences are cohesive and progressive.

When we finally depart our period in history and return to the wellspring of all reality, will we be ready to meet our other selves or would we prefer to read about them in a book? Only you can decide.

18

How Are Soul Mates and Families Chosen? Do We Live with Them after We Die or Do They Go Back to Live with People of Their Own "Level"?

It's quite common to hear in metaphysical circles that people get to choose their families before incarnating. In that sense, there is a version of "destiny" being played out, as both sets of personalities—parents and children—make these arrangements ahead of Time (pun intended). However, no matter how long this belief has circulated, I wasn't ready to necessarily buy into it strictly on faith.

Family bonds and dynamics are fascinating, with twists, turns, quirks, and upsets which oftentimes cannot be predicted. And as some of these events unfold, you inevitably ask yourself, "If I really do choose my family, why did I choose this bunch?" This notion becomes even more upsetting when we are in families of violence, sexual trauma, or otherwise incredibly harsh circumstances, which require years of therapy to even cope. Who would want to exist in a family like that by choice? Especially if we can see such trauma from a No-Time perspective?

Admittedly, it is hard to accept. However, as revealed by the Interviews, family relationships are not "one time only." Families stick together through many time periods simultaneously—although occasionally switching out who is playing what role (parent, child, grandparent) in order to work through lessons or balancing out karmic energies coexisting through the other simultaneous reincarnational selves. And sometimes, these energies can be extreme...

When we consider the fact that in death we cannot take anything with us, all we are left with are our relationships with others. Those bonds, those memories of closeness or of harshness, are our attachments to relationships that we carry with us from here to the Other Side. And as mentioned above, not all relationships are pleasant—and you'd best be aware that you take those memories with you, too (they'll get played out in the Life Review). The inequities within these bonds don't go away by the shedding of the physical world; they are some of the things we actually do take with us. Let's begin with Michael from session one:

> He says, "*I have a lot of serious issues to work out, so when it came to choosing my family, I did it with intense seriousness.*" He's making me feel like, "*I'll be doing it again later.*" He's still coming from a perspective of a future self...He says, "*In the future, with the family relationships, I will be equally as serious, but I think next time I will put just a little bit of lightheartedness in there.*"

Here, Michael concedes that he had relationship issues coming into his life and that these have since carried over for which a potential future self (or series of future selves) will work to balance out. The transcript continued:

> He shows me a picture of four or five blobs, possibly relating to his issues. "*It was because of the issues which I knew I needed to work on, that I choose the family the way I did.*" He says, "*Understand that it is an agreement between everybody involved...And that it goes both ways...It's a two-way street, everyone is getting something out of the relationship.*"

In session two, Jodi's ex-husband, Ock, also related that he, too, had problems with certain members of the family. However, he acknowledged the reality of having chosen to be with these people who brought him friction:

> He says, "*Yes, I even chose those family members that did not like me and that I did not get along with. But at the time you*

make these choices, you understand the gains and the losses that are going to occur through the nature of the relationship." He says, *"You do formulate the pattern and everything. You can go into…not necessarily liking it…but it is still your choice, because you understand what the parties are going to get out of it."*

Notice how he mentioned that people understood the gains and losses that were available to everyone by reincarnating together. This was a recurring theme as to why certain family members still chose to be around one another, even if they didn't necessarily get along. From Debbie's father in session seven:

He starts pulling taffy, as if to say, *"We need some of these people in our experiences to pull and shape us. We have certain goals and aspirations in mind when we go through the drama of life, so we sometimes need these people to mold us and shape us in the directions we aspire to. Some of us prefer to grow by having the head-banging opportunity versus…For some people it's easier to engrain the lessons and stuff when they have to struggle with them as opposed to just having them handed to you."*

According to Gabi's mother, even though some relationships challenge us, the design to come together and the reasons behind it are from the very nature of love:

She says, *"With love, even those people you don't get along with, the reason you come together is really a reason of love. Sometimes love requires a little challenge in order for it to work. You're doing it to expand…"*

This was exemplified by the spirit of Rose, who had been married and divorced multiple times throughout her life. While she was in her elderly years, it was a source of amusement because she was so wild and free. In the Interview, she wasn't afraid to talk about her past loves and the challenges, intimating it was all out of love, even during the trying times:

She says, "*This is why I had so many marriages.*" She says, "*I have been with these guys in previous lifetimes, and some of these relationships were so tumultuous, up and down, up and down.*" Nothing was ever smooth for her…She just keeps showing me all these past incarnations and with all these guys, her husbands, and it's like a big juggling act. She says, "*I have been around the block with these guys so many times.*" And she says, "*I have gotten used to them being around me. I wanted them to be around me.*" And she's making me feel like, there is this notion that you are getting together to bring balance and work things out that happened in the past, but ultimately, "*I wanted the relationships. I wanted them around.*" It's what she wanted. In saying that, she's making me feel like, "*Indeed, we choose the relationships that we bring into our lives. That there is this glue…*" She shows it to me like a rubber cement, because you can stretch it but it always bounces back. This was the nature of the relationships. "*When you set out, all you have are relationships. When you come back to the earth sphere, you want to bring those relationships with you. And they want to come back too. So why not?*"

Diane in session fourteen further explained how families are chosen based on the cooperative nature of each individual's needs. She said families are "chosen based on the needs and lessons of each person that comes together." From her point of view, the family collection has to do with the journeys that each person is taking.

Sarah's wise grandfather really summed up the whole thing. He not only explained why families stick together, he also revealed that not all members of the group create friction due to karma:

He's showing me different levels in the family, as if to say, "*There are certain people in the family that you don't necessarily like to have in your circle, but they are there because of the growth experiences, and the challenges that they provide to make you grow in certain areas and directions you want and that you need for the purpose of reincarnation.*" And he's saying, "*Some of these people that challenge us can belong to our inner circle and are just playing a role and we are ignorant of that fact while alive here."*

But he also went on to describe those that do sometimes bother us and why we choose to have them surround us in other incarnations:

"There are some people in the family that really are not of your inner circle, but you have had dealings with in the past, so you are balancing out these relationships that you may have had prior that may have had issues, problems, things out of balance...inequality, inequality." He says, *"When you go through the Life Review, and you understand your injustices to others, it is a natural reaction for you to want to repair that injustice with that person; and to do it in a much more meaningful way than to just say 'I'm sorry.' You want to make it a vital, physical, emotional, and spiritual connection of forgiveness. The only way you can do that...is through engaging them through these processes."* He's making me feel like, *"Yes, you could change that nature of the relationship in the spiritual realm, but some people come from the perspective of since they got messed up down on earth, that is where we need to correct it; that's where the balance will come in; they have to have the balance in the same dynamic in the same areas. Some people will have these reincarnational experiences to provide these experiences to bring balance."*

So when the drama of life is over and all members of the circle have returned to the Other Side, the acknowledgement of the relationships is recognized. However, this doesn't mean "all is forgiven" and family who couldn't stand being around one another on earth are suddenly embracing in unbridled joy in heaven. This is why some people stay in interaction with these same personalities in other incarnations. Debbie's father in session seven explained it to me like this:

"With some people, you choose to reincarnate in a family structure in order to balance out the energies, the injustices, that sort

of thing." He says "*It's a very strange thing when you're in a No-Time zone to realize that there are parts of you that are currently out in the Time zone going through this orchestra...to make all of these...to experience all of these things...*" He is making me feel like it's an orchestration...It's an orchestration...You've got a whole big band thing going on...but it's out here in Time and you're existing in No-Time. "*It's a trip, it's a trip.*"

Nancy's father from session three had this to say:

> He says families are chosen intentionally...You make all those connections. And he's making me feel like, at one point in time in some other existence, he was your kid and you were the adult. He turns himself into a baby and places himself down at your feet. So he's talking about roles being played; that you do circulate around one another.

In like fashion, those family members that we had close ties to, we tend to still hang around with. All-in-all, it's really quite *flexible*. Those we like to be with we will continue to have in our lives on the Other Side. The others...Well, family reunions only happen every so often, right? And for good reason. This isn't to say people (for the most part) are on different "levels" of evolution, we just don't always mesh with other "frequencies." As Michael put it from session one:

> He says, "*For those people who have bad marriages, they don't necessarily go to different levels, but they will split apart and they will maintain their own separate individual identities and lives and regrets...And hopefully the time apart in this other world will help makes things better with them.*" He also says they will maintain the same friends, too.

From Grace's grandmother in session four:

> She says, "*When we die, we will meet and greet various family members. But based on certain lessons and pools of energies,*

some will stay together and hang around together, while others may go off in different directions. While they were on earth, points needed to be made, references needed to be explained; that once the lifetime is over, has been accomplished, they could then separate."

Diane in session fourteen went on to describe the union on the Other Side as being quite dynamic. Love is still expressed, as each person unites in a family for certain reasons; but that doesn't necessarily mean it is all hugs and kisses. She impressed upon me:

She's making me feel like, getting back together on the Other Side is a personal decision. Some will come back together because they were close; but for those that weren't close on earth, it doesn't mean they will now be close on the Other Side. It's per the individual.

She says, *"There's always an acknowledgement of the relationship between people, even if it's a far away type of relationship; the acknowledgement of the relationship is still there because you are interconnected in that way, but you don't have to like everybody."*

She says you're dealing with different frequencies and journeys...The love for everybody comes in the sense of you servicing them on their journey...So there is this notion of all love between everything. Then she says other people's journeys are on a different radio station frequency...So if she's jazz, yet one of her siblings is rock and roll, she will—out of love— service them on their journey for a portion of it...and get help in return. But because she is not a rock and roll person, she is not going to hang with them. It's not suitable for both of them to do that. They will come together to help each other in their journeys in their small ways, but they don't need to stay locked together. She says it's not like a marriage.

Cynthia's father from session five echoed the theme:

He says for the most part, the family groups stay together. He's making me feel like…There are some family circles where there will be members who drop in from other different "levels" but they aren't really too much higher from everybody else's levels, but they do bring some kind of a knowledge that the other members of the circle don't have. *"Knowledge and being,"* he says, *"wrap up 'being' with that word."* So there would be certain other members of the family that would stand out if you were to place everybody in a circle. He says, *"Yeah they hang out with us, but they are kind of a little bit up above the rest of the circle. That's because you need certain people in the group to inspire growth, and inspire change. But that doesn't make them gods or anything. It's not like that at all. Nobody is ever parallel…you will have people that are up and down."*

Gabi's mother in session thirteen went on to describe a notion of levels within the family structure:

She says depending on the dynamics of the family, there are certain family members that are on a different perceived "level" than you are, and they will go back there. But they will have been altered by the very nature of the relationship in the life they had with the other family members. Everyone is progressing; everyone is on this course of evolution. And it all works. She says, *"Family members (no matter where you go over there, because 'levels' really are not all that great between people) can visit other people (unless that other person was a very diabolical person). For the most part, family members are close enough in energy frequency; you can visit them."*

There are some people that are really bonded…Like you and your mother…The two of you will remain close over there. She says, *"There are some family members that aren't that way… Like the black sheep of the family. You will probably connect, but then they will go off and do their own thing."*

The spirits kept saying that family units were created with intimate details and patterns in mind. When one exists in a No-Time zone, it appears careful planning can be skillfully executed over the entire span of the lifetime on earth. That is, something that can occur in life whether one be as young as five, fifteen, or even eighty years of age can be considered "orchestrated" from the field of No-Time. This may sound like "destiny" or "fate," or what some have referred to as "contracts." I personally don't like the idea of any of these, for it insinuates that we don't have free will on certain occasions. Although, perhaps in a sense, that is sometimes functionally true, as demonstrated by Marti's mother in session ten. Earlier in the Life Review, she had mentioned that during one of the painful times in her life she had to disappoint a male suitor who had asked her to marry him. When this question of designing families came about, she brought my awareness back to that moment with the other man. Here's how it came out in the transcript:

> Earlier, remember how she mentioned the one guy she dumped? She makes me feel like, "*Had I not dumped him, you would not have been born.*" I think that what she's getting at; there was just something in her consciousness which knew he wasn't the right one because of everything else that was coming down the road. She didn't know it consciously, but it's one of those things that may have driven the whole thing. She's making me feel like, the connection with your father was pre-ordained in some way. That relationship had to come together in order for things to be made manifest. In that sense, there are certain relationships that are key—she's literally showing me a key—there are key relationships that are destiny; they have to happen.

The conversation revealed how everyone in the family had a hand in creating the design, as well as the dynamics. This was echoed by other spirits who came through the sessions, such as Grace's grandmother in session four:

She makes me feel like, "*We all choose the family; we all choose the dynamics of the life we live.*" Meaning that before you were born, the dynamic of her taking care of you as your grand-mother and your biological parents being somewhat out of the picture was already a part of the plan, it was already in the dynamic. She says, "*We choose our parents and our family more succinctly...like seeds we plant in the ground for the gar-den we want to grow.*"

This notion of being "grown" was further brought out eight sessions later, from Kourtnie's father:

He says, "*Families are grown...*" I think what he means is that... The family unit is a structure that is put into place around the time one incarnates. There are intricate lines that have to come together to make the whole family unit materialize, and this is what he means by it is grown. He's making me feel like, "*We as a family had pasts together with these other lives and so we had to come together...*"

Part of the original question to this chapter included an idea about "levels." There is a concept that consciousness exists in a progressive state of evolution, and in the spiritual realm, some spirits have advanced in evolution to a higher state and would be perceived to exist on a "higher" level. In conjunction with this idea is a sense that these other levels are not necessarily accessible lest one have the right knowledge or aspect of consciousness already in place. We will spend more time on this concept in the next few chapters, but I wanted to hint at it in this one to see what the spirits might have to say regarding the family structure and how the idea of an evolutionary consciousness ladder played out among the fam-ily. Here's what Terri's grandmother Rose had to say:

She says, "*I believe there is such a thing as a level in terms of how much somebody knows and what that knowledge can produce for them.*" But she's like, everybody at least for her, everybody that she hung around with, all of her husbands, she's saying the difference between levels was small. Yes, there were some people that were higher than her, and some people that were a little bit lower, *"but because we can all relate to one another, we're all on similar wavelengths."* It doesn't mean they have to get along. It just means, that there is not such a gap between levels that one person was just a complete saint next to her. *"We were all kind of close together,"* she says. Your relationships don't go away, is what she's really making me feel. No matter how high up or down on a level they might be, you are close enough together that you are still able to communicate and interact and belong to each other. She's making me feel like, a lot of the people that she's with, there's this sense of belonging with them.

From Nancy's father in session three:

> When it comes to the levels thing…He acknowledges that certain members of the group will have…different "proclivities"…Different proclivities that sort of separate them from other members of the family…But in relation to a hierarchical sort of thing…where some person is one level above another…He says they are really very close. There are some that are a little bit higher than the others, but nothing that would make them really separate from…There's close things going on. He's making me feel like certain issues that are being worked out similarly between a lot of members…not everybody, but a good portion of the circle.

And from Cynthia's father in session five:

> There are some family circles where there will be members who drop in from other different "levels" but they aren't really too much higher from everybody else; yet they do bring some kind of a knowledge in that the other members of the circle don't have.

When it comes to incarnating with certain lessons and intentions, as well as expertise or proclivities that can engage, inspire, or move others along on their intended path, we can begin to see why we gravitate around certain people or momentarily "hook up" with others. Family ties, it seems, are oftentimes much deeper than what surface awareness grants us. Though none of the spirits came right out and said it, I feel after having listened to these Interviews and observed many family dynamics (my own included), groups of people come together with similar themes—learning self-reliance, self-love, or letting go of certain blockages. Some will succeed, others will fail, others will evolve only slightly, but the group is really working on similar issues. Those similarities and themes would be impetus for how we "design" the makeup of the family unit— who would be parents, children, grandchildren, and how the roles would play off of one another.

In other cases, we choose certain family members precisely because of the challenges they instill within us. These challenges can be for a variety of reasons: balancing conflict and energy through the parties as they exist with simultaneous selves spread out through the prism of linear Time; to forcing us by virtue of the discord to realize greater truths which we would otherwise miss without the dissonance. We may not like interacting with certain family members, but our intuition, our higher selves, put us together for a reason and we must sometimes relent to this wisdom and "suffer through it," knowing on some level that it serves a greater purpose. Once life has run its course and personalities return to the non-physical No-Time realm, we can reflect on our relationships from this world and decide if we wish to hang out with those family members on the Other Side. Although each soul will remain in his or her own sense of personhood, some may still decide to reside elsewhere, apart from the old family. Some may even move on to a different "sphere of activity" altogether. But the relationships will forever remain.

19

Are There Such Things as Levels—a Hierarchy for Those That Are More or Less Evolved Based on Some Aspect of Either Time or Expansion? Can We Know Our Level or Do We Need To?

We briefly touched upon this subject in the last chapter. Nevertheless, I definitely wanted to devote a whole chapter to this idea, as I was quite curious about it when designing the questions. When I think about the purpose of existence and apply a notion of evolution to the concept of life, it does make one think that perhaps there might be a spiritual "ladder of progression." If so, what would the spirits tell us about it? First, I wanted to see if they could *confirm* the notion of a progressive scale to begin with. If so, what could they reveal? How does one progress from one level to the next? How do the levels differ? Are they predefined like floors on a skyscraper? Could someone legitimately say, "There are twenty-four levels to the spirit world"? If there are predefined levels, is it possible to know which level we are currently on?

As was typical with most questions, the answers I received from the multitude of spirits were unique to each individual, yet they also revealed some commonalities. Admittedly, the notion of spiritual levels is an abstract idea, and so the responses given by the spirits were more or less symbolic and representational, and perhaps not so literal. In other words, it's all a matter of perception, and I did my best to convey each spirit's message as clearly as I could.

When we first think in terms of levels, our mind conjures the image of a ladder, each rung representing advancement in consciousness. Yet this was not how it was described to me by some of the spirits. Here's how Ock from session two described spirit evolution:

> He says, "*Yeah, there's this whole consciousness thing... this development of consciousness...*" He's making me feel like it's about the evolvement, evolution, expansion of spirit...He doesn't like the word "*spirit*"...it's consciousness. It's about becoming the biggest balloon that you can, and filling the balloon—the air is knowledge, wisdom, practical experience. He says that's what it's about. "*If you're going to give levels, this is what the level thing really means—it's the big balloon.*"

Diane from session fourteen also tied spiritual evolution to the nature of consciousness, and was able to give a fascinating context for it within the dynamics of the spirit world:

> She's making me feel like, it's not levels...it is awareness, knowledge of consciousness. She says, "*Time has nothing to do with it because Time is meaningless.*" The closest is the word "expansion" but she places the word "consciousness" over that. In placing the word "consciousness" over it, she's saying it is an awareness of the fullness of consciousness. She's also spelling the word "experience." So she's saying it is the experiential awareness of consciousness. She says, "*You are to be the experiential awareness of consciousness—and you can't do that in one round.*" She is saying, "*We are aware this is what it is. But nobody is doing the 'I'm better than you because I have fuller awareness.' There isn't any finger pointing.*" She says, "*Because people want to experience their own consciousness in their own way, they want to develop it in their own way, so... it has nothing to do with good or bad. Those are labels. Everything just IS. Just IS.*"

From Terri K.'s brother in session nine:

He wouldn't call it levels like a step ladder...He's drawing it more like a bubble. The bubble is the environment. He says, *"It's based on your awareness of that environment, but there's interaction."*

From Marti's mother in session ten:

She doesn't like the word "levels", but she does say the word *"ascension"*... rising up. She's making me feel like, it's not rungs of a ladder, but there is this moving up ascension having to do with energy. She's making me feel like it's very organic, it's very natural, it's not anything incredibly...It's not like a building, is what she's showing me, such as you stop at floor three, then you go up to floor four. To me, she says it all runs together, but there is an ascension in the progression.

The more the spirits talked, the more they made it sound like there really weren't any kind of levels, per se; it was just what amount of knowledge a spirit had which either allowed it to accomplish certain tasks or kept itself challenged. Here's how Cynthia's father from session five described it:

He wants to take the word *"level"* and turn it into, *"awareness of your heart."* He says it has to do with the awareness of your heart...He wants to use that as the gauge for levels. He's saying, *"Depending on where you know where you are in your heart— knowing determines the course and nature of your existence."* He's making me feel like there is no map or roadway...There is no predefined roadway...It has to do with how much you know inside, which will determine your course in the nature of your experience.

From Sarah's grandfather in session six:

He says, *"At one point in your life you couldn't drive a car, but your parents knew eventually you would, so it wasn't that driving a car was ever held from you, it was always there, you just hadn't grown into it yet. That's what this whole thing is, in terms of a level question. Nothing is being held back, nothing is being kept secret from you, you just haven't grown into it yet."*

The whole education theme really played out in the Interviews, especially from Kourtnie's father in session twelve:

He says make it like college, where you can get an education that just happens to be more knowledgeable than someone else right next to you, but not necessarily as knowledgeable as the next person in line. And when you apply education to the working world, you can get certain jobs because you have the education, but you can't get certain jobs if you don't. He says if you have knowledge, you have energy; there's this combination with it. He says if you have it, you can do certain things with it that certain others can't. But it doesn't mean anybody is better than anybody else…it's just where you're at.

Gabi's mother in session thirteen had this to say:

She says the whole levels thing is a mental thing that you ascribe to yourself. She says, *"You can look at your neighbor who thinks he's at this level, when you would perceive him more at this level. The level thing is a personal judgment you are putting on yourself in regard to where you think you should be in the course of your development."* She says, *"No one is judging you in the course of your development."* She says, *"It's all about energy; it's all about how energy works and the dynamics of energy."*

It was a very important point that the spirits wanted to make regarding the question: there was no judgment as to where people thought they were in the course of their evolution. In today's society, we love to think of people in a hierarchical scale, with those on top considered the "haves" while those beneath the "have less" to "have nots." Along with this judgment comes a sense of superiority or inferiority—depending on where you think you reside along this continuum. In the spiritual world, however, wherever you are on this evolutionary scale is worthwhile and no one judges you for it. From Sarah's grandfather in session six:

> He understands the concepts of levels, but he does this with it...He draws this line up here and brushes the under-stuff away. He says, "*You are always up here on top. This whole idea of being lesser than or whatever is completely wrong. It's not right, it's not the way things are.*"

From Kourtnie's father in session twelve:

> He says this is paradoxical...He shows me this idea of a hierarchy, but he says, "*Don't make it out to be this big, heavy, important stuff. It doesn't mean you're less than this person up here, or that you're more than this person down here.*"

Although levels weren't being clearly defined or delineated, the spirits did acknowledge that certain wisdom of experience granted certain capacities or abilities within the spirit world. From Gabi's mother in session thirteen:

> She says, "*Where you are at in there (in terms of a level) does determine certain functions, abilities, things you can see and do.*" She says it's like tying your shoe. You can't run in your shoes until you learn to tie them, so there may be steps or levels you may not have reached to be able to do certain things—but it's not a judgment thing. No one is saying, "*You suck because you're not at this level.*"

Since it appears there aren't any definable rungs on this consciousness ladder, it would be impossible to determine just "where" we reside individually, for there wouldn't be any frame of reference.

In the end, since all Time is simultaneous, the spirits acknowledged the Oversoul as having the expansion of the entire spectrum; it was only the individual fragments that lacked certain perceptions to that reality.

Debbie's father, in session seven, gave an illustration of that concept:

> For him…He says when you're in the No-Time zone and you
> see these other incarnations, you instantly become aware of
> an idea of levels…However in No-Time, since you're seeing all
> of this, you also get this notion that it's already completed…
> Whatever these levels are, they're already done. It's just some-
> how…wrapping your awareness around that and into that. He
> says, "*On earth, you really don't know your level*"…He says you
> judge and compare based on economic lifestyle on earth, and
> that's no basis for determining a spiritual level or the growth of
> the entity. For some reason, he's remaining at a certain point
> of view, versus an omniscient completed awareness, which he
> understands is going on in a No-Time zone.
>   Practicing patience…He's saying…there's just so much to
> it, and it's so "wow" that you wouldn't just want to all of a sud-
> den "go to the end." There's so much awesomeness to life, from
> the perspective of where's he at, that he doesn't require or feel
> the need to abandon his position. He doesn't feel like he's an
> invalid person because of all of the others.

Clearly, Debbie's father was saying that the validity of one's life was not dependent upon where someone stood on a spiritual level. He was quite right in suggesting that we on earth would most likely "judge" someone were we to be aware of what "rung" someone would be standing on. In this sense, maybe it was wise that the spirits weren't telling me what separates one level from another—or if there is any separation at all. Nevertheless, the concept of expansion and ascension continued to wind its way through the Interviews, and how it all played out in the field of No-Time, as evidenced by Marti's mother in session ten:

> From her point of view you will ascend, you will go up. She's
> giving me the word "*particle*"…Okay, she wants to get into the
> reincarnational selves…In some respects, your reincarnational
> selves already encompass this ascension. So there are parts of
> you that are already up and parts of you that are already down.

But because these are imbued with a sense of individualization even though you are connected, they're still considered…not necessarily a separate entity, but they are individualized. It's like the fingers on your hand…They are separate fingers, yet comprise the wholeness of the hand.

Terri's grandmother, Rose, gave a different analogy to try and explain the nature of expansion:

She doesn't want to break it down into levels, like a level one, level two, level three. She's making me feel like, it's more spread out. She doesn't like the feel of a ladder, like you're stuck on a ladder, and then you move to the next rung, and the next rung. She says, *"Energy exists on a spectrum. In that spectrum you can go up or down, slower or faster."* She's saying, *"You don't get into a car and go from zero to five miles an hour, and then jump immediately to sixty without going six miles an hour up to fifty-nine."* She says that's why the ladder rung thing doesn't work. You can't use that as an analogy. Because like a speedometer, you have to go through the other speeds to reach sixty. It's like a smooth progression, not one that hops. There are some people on what would be considered a lower level (lesser speed zone) and others will be higher, but it's all interconnected.

Gabi's mother in session thirteen went on to describe why judgement does not exist when it came to the idea of expansion:

She says love is really the goal because that encompasses everything; it embraces everything. And everything is One in that expression. So really what you're working on is that expression.

To sum up, the whole idea of "levels" like a ladder is a misnomer to most spirits. Apparently there are energy frequencies—and awareness seems to play a part in which frequency one exists. And these frequencies allow for certain abilities or functionalities over others, yet no one is judged based upon what frequency they exist in. This freedom from judgment stems from the idea that at some point in the frequency domain, another portion of the Oversoul for which a lower vibrational personality is existing is also balanced out by a self existing in a higher frequency range. Grace's grandmother explained it like this:

> She doesn't make it levels; she wants to make it a landscape, as if to say there are certain people who have traversed deeper across the landscape than others. And in doing that, going deeper across the landscape, they've learned more. She doesn't like the idea of posing it like a ladder, with people above other people. She doesn't want to make it feel like that. She wants to make it feel like some people have more experience than others, so that gains them more knowledge or wisdom. She says in terms of people being wiser and having more wisdom because of where they have traveled, yes; but she says that doesn't negate the value or the worth of the people that are back here because it's known that these people will also be up here at some point in their journey.
>
> The amount of distance traveled is delineated by the experience one derives from life (whether on earth or in the spirit world), the education from it...That determines the distance. She's showing me a body and filling it up like a bottle of wine, and is making me feel like, "*Okay, these people have poured more wine into their body from their experiences. They drank more from their lives...It's the filling up.*"

In other words, do not worry about where you exist on this abstract scale—wherever you are, this particular frequency is important and filled with immense value. As you progress, you will learn more of who and what you are, and will, in turn, be able to do more. But never negate who and where you are right now. In the grand scheme, you are already complete; you are already *perfect*.

20

How Do We Advance If There Are Levels? Are We Limited in a Life as to How Many Levels We Can Proceed? Do We Advance in the Spiritual Realm as Well as the Physical?

As we learned from the last question, there aren't really levels per se, in how evolution is gauged; nor is there a ladder with pre-defined rungs defining where someone is on a consciousness scale. However, that still doesn't negate the idea of evolution and some sort of advancement. This question helped flesh out an even greater picture of life's purpose, whether living here on earth or on the Other Side. In a few cases, the spirits went along with the concept of levels, if only because it was the metaphor I was using. For others, they completely dismissed the notion and replaced it for something more holistic.

In all cases, the spirits were unanimous in stating that advancement proceeds, whether alive on earth or on the Other Side. And just because we move from one place to the other doesn't mean personal evolution gets a turbo boost either, as expressed by Cynthia's father in session five:

> He says expansion is inherent in every place you are at, so even there in the spirit world, they are advancing. He's making me feel like, *"But don't think our expansion is any more advanta-geous because of where we're at versus your own."* He's making me feel like, *"No, no, no, it's pretty much equal…"* He's saying, *"No, it's definitely equal because it all pertains to the personality and the individual."*

Sarah's grandfather from session six concurred:

> Yes, he says we advance in both realms. The first part of the question, the notion of being small and then "boom!" growing into this large spiritual being, no. He says it's a gradual thing. *"It's your life, you know your speed and how you progress. You don't instantly blow up, amazingly shooting forward and becoming massively awesome. It just doesn't happen. But it's timed to your own view of progression, your own sense of progression,"* is what he's making me feel. He says, *"As long as you are enjoying and engaging life, you will progress."*

Terri's grandmother Rose had this to say:

> Her answer is, *"Just live your life. Just live your life."* She makes me feel that it is inherent you will advance. Do we advance in the spiritual world as well as the physical? She's making me feel like, yes, even though you are outside the body you don't stop learning. You don't stop growing. She doesn't want to make it this big magical storybook. And she's making me feel like, when it comes to evolution, that the evolution of consciousness ascending the ladder, she's acknowledging that we would perceive it as something being very slow. But when you're in the No-Time zone...there's this sense of peace with it; that it's all okay, that it all works out. *"You just live your life."*

A few of the spirits again tried to show an analogy to explain the concept of spiritual evolution, since the idea of a ladder simply wasn't appropriate. Between the last question and this one, Nancy's father from session three backed out and was replaced by the spirit of Nancy's sister, Katie. Again, after taking some time to get pertinent data to validate the mediumship connection, Katie went on to answer this question:

> She's putting me in a car and going down the road...going down the...and talks about the journey. And puts potholes in the road...As soon as you ask, "How do we advance?," she

goes "Boom!" and drops me into a pothole. So, she's saying, from her point of view, the advancement is the potholes...getting in and getting out. Those are the lessons. But she makes sure the road is flat as opposed to hilly. The road is all right there for you...maybe not to be seen fully...but you understand that it's not hard...It's not a hill you have to put a lot of power into, you just have to get through the potholes. She says the road is always there, you're just driving the course...

Now she says, "*When it comes to the potholes, if you're bright enough, you can navigate around them. The whole life thing, coming here and living these hard lessons, you don't have to do that. It doesn't have to be that way. It's a road, and you can travel around the potholes if you want to.*" She says most people don't want to...She is saying that some people feel...a natural pull to go into the potholes. It just grabs them and pulls them in. But you don't have to do that.

Advance in spiritual realm as well as physical...She says, "*Yes, yes, yes, most surely you do.*" She says, "*Even though you may die, you don't stop living. And living is the process of driving down the road.*"

Grace's grandmother from session four had this to say:

She says you naturally advance on your own, by living...Then she backs up and says, "*Let me clarify for a bit...When you go out with your eyes open and your ears open and your heart open and your mind open, you will take in and see everything, and you will be able to process the magnitude of everything. And when you're able to do that, and concentrate, and gain the pearls of wisdom from doing that...You will move down the road.*" She says, "*By contrast, there are some people who can't do that. They can only do little bits at a time, they either don't see or they don't hear, or they block some kind of sense, or they do take it in and don't sit with it—they just flush it right out as soon as it comes in.*" She holds them as if to say their movement is so dang slow...

She says, the reason it's so slow, is because they don't understand they're wrapped up with everything; that they are a part of everything and everything a part of them. When you start to realize that, and you start to work and orchestrate with that, you can begin to move down this road to becoming a better being and having a better understanding of what all life is.

Here, Grace's grandmother expressed that each person's pace through the evolutionary process will be individual. That is, some will advance more quickly than others. But as stated in the previous chapter, no one judges anybody based on their perceived current level or path. This was again echoed by the spirits in regard to this question. From Michael in session one:

He says, "*There is nobody prodding you...nobody prodding you saying, 'You need to go two levels' or 'Get moving...get up there.' It's all at your own speed.*"

From Sarah's grandfather in session six:

He says, "*Some people may choose to rush it, but some people don't because they know—all time being simultaneous or non-existent—you're already there.*" He says it's beautiful to smell the roses.

From Debbie's father in session seven:

He says consciousness is wrapped up as its own cause, so there is no right or wrong to it; development is wholly dependent upon the individual. He is making me feel like, "*When you realize your scope in the great being (the Oversoul) you attain awareness of your eternal spark as each individual...Also obtaining its own unique globular reality...Disassociate from one person being lower or higher than another, because all of those levels are You in the No-Time zone.*"

And this from M.G.'s mother in session eight:

> She's making me feel like, don't think of it as levels. *"Levels present a psychological idea of a ladder you have to climb and struggle against."* She says it's not like that at all. *"You are where you are based on awareness. It doesn't mean you are any less of a person or anything like that...There's no right or wrongness to where you're at..."*
>
> She's showing me a body filling out, as if to say, *"All you're doing is filling out your potentials...your beingness. Don't get caught up in this idea you have to be in a certain frame or type. We all go through this, it's part of the function, and it's part of the reality."*

So just what exactly does it mean to advance? In the last chapter we learned that it had to do with awareness, and that new awareness brought new possibilities in terms of abilities and things which could be done. As the spirits kept saying—you can't run until you learn to walk. In answering this question, the spirits alluded to what helped or hindered one's growth process: the beliefs, feelings, and attitudes one harbored. Let's start with Kourtnie's father from session twelve:

> He says in heaven, to give the perception of moving up, in order to move up, you've got to get out of your head. *"You have to get off your ass and get out of your own goddamn way."* And what he's showing me are logs that are blocking the flow of water and he's making me feel like these logs are crap. This is the crap you hold onto in your mind about how the universe should work for you, and who you think you really are. He says, *"When you let that go, and you let the water flow, and you understand that it's not you against the universe, that it's the two of you working together, that is when advancement takes place."*

From Gabi's mother in session thirteen:

> She is like, "*Once you abandon the idea of levels and accept that
> it is expression and working with energy, you can go wherever
> you want to.*" Then she says, "*When you are on earth, because
> of all the mental constructs we create, all this brainwashing...*"
> She takes mental ideas and throws them down like wooden
> blocks to impede one from moving...She says, "*On earth, if
> you would just get out of your head, you would have a much
> better time with life.*" But...because of these things on earth
> we do, the ability to advance... she would rather use the word
> "alter"..."*In order to alter your energy to go in these other areas
> of direction would be a whole lot easier if you didn't have these
> mental blocks to deal with.*"

Here, Gabi's mother tried to keep focused on the concept of a person being
an energy frequency and how advancement affected a person's energy,
thus providing more possibilities.

Sometimes, just being closed-minded and under the spell of the ego
can also inhibit a sense of expansion, as related by Terri K.'s brother in my
ninth sitting:

> He is showing me that people do a lot of...not necessarily
> looking to expand...but more looking back into themselves...
> Narcissistic point of view. He says there are so many people
> who keep going back into themselves instead of acknowledg-
> ing they could expand out here and not lose anything about
> who and what they are. He's saying, admittedly, it's tougher
> when you're in the body because you lose access to points of
> view that come more easily when you're outside the body, but
> you're still able to engage the whole process and experience it.

Then, of course, we wonder about the nature of our simultaneous reincarnational selves. Do they play a part in any of this expansion? It
would be foolish to assume they didn't. Alas, the spirits made me feel like
the earthly experience, when wrapped up with multiple selves, is one way
of engaging in growth and advancement. No doubt, the earthly realm
with its challenges and stressors, as well as joys, can be an excellent envi-

ronment to temper someone's soul. It is in this crucible that some spirits find the nature of evolution to be more appreciated and experienced versus working on it in the spiritual world, as was expressed by Michael in session one:

> He shows me that there are some people that really do get so complacent with the spiritual land, that they are completely content to live there and do the same thing over and over again with the idea of "*I'm going to reincarnate now, I'm going to reincarnate now,*" and therefore their advancement is very slow.

Of course, this predisposes someone continuing to view his existence in a linear time frame, or who is willing to "pass the buck" to another portion of himself living the earthly experience. Admittedly, to place the bulk of evolution in the earthly realm instead of the spiritual gives the perception of evolutionary advancement as being a slow process, though Time really has no meaning in the greater scheme, as expressed by Diane in session fourteen:

> She says it is always expansion whether it's here or there. It's always about expansion. And because Time is meaningless, she's making me feel like, "*You shouldn't worry about where you're at, so long as you are engaged in being the best person you can be. That is the only directive.*"

Grace's grandmother went on to describe how reincarnation could be considered more or less a "tool" in how one can continue to evolve:

> She says the majority of people will utilize the reincarnation technique...technology...for the advancement. She says certain people are in love with the whole physical world and that is their preferred method of filling themselves out and going down the landscape. Then she says there are people here who have "graduated"—her term—from the idea of needing to do it that way. So you can continue to develop and go down the

landscape without having to take on another body. Yes, evolution never stops. It's a big ball that keeps rolling.

Marti's mother in session ten further expanded on this notion:

> Okay, she wants to get into the reincarnational selves...She says, *"In some respects, your reincarnational selves already encompass this ascension."* So there are parts of you that are already up and parts of you that are already down. But because these are imbued with a sense of individualization even though you are connected, they're still considered a...not necessarily a separate entity, but they are individualized. She's making me feel like the individuation factor has to do with experience, of owning experience, and even though you may have reincarnational selves up there (on the ascension ladder) it's still their experience and not your own. It's like giving the hints and clues to the totality of being, but until you experience it, all you have is a hint or a clue and not the experiential side of it.

Ultimately, one can imagine each of our simultaneous reincarnational selves encompassing all parts of this energetic frequency ladder of evolution. Though we are connected in various ways, filling out the high and lows of this ladder, we are still individual and certain perceptions may block us from realizing this grand orchestration. Nevertheless, the key is to continue imbuing one's self with more and more experiences so that we get to become fuller beings and understand it in a multidimensional way. In becoming fuller beings, we get to do and become more with our abilities in conjunction with the universe.

As to the second part of this question—"Are we limited in a life as to how many levels we can proceed?"—the answers were all the same. Mainly, if we are going to use the concept of levels, we must acknowledge each "location" as having an abundance of potentials and possibilities to be explored. Several spirits encouraged my sitters and me to "Take your time and smell the roses." It's not a race to get to the top; nor can one reach heightened levels without proper knowledge and experience to support them.

In the end, advancement in a single lifetime was considered small, in terms of increments. Again, without predefined levels and things that define each level from another, it's impossible to say how "far" someone could evolve, but the consensus was "not too far." From Michael in session one:

> "*As for moving multiple levels, that would be quite the feat in the physical world...There's so much...*" He's making me feel like that down here on earth, it's such a base frequency, it's so dense, it would be a miracle to really go beyond...He says you can definitely advance into the next level, but going above and beyond that, pretty unlikely."

From session four, with the spirit of Grace's grandmother:

> Limited as to distance? She's making me feel like, "*No, but it's so wide and so vast that you would never be able to traverse three or four of them at one time, one place, one event, one journey. You can jump one, maybe two, but there's so much involved in a landscape, so much to take in.*" She makes it feel like, it's such a wonderful thing and joyous thing—there's so much to enjoy in every landscape, don't feel like you have to rush it.

Cynthia's father in session five added this:

> The environment itself, yes, it has its clues and its advantages, but the speed of which somebody advances is still predicated on the individual personality's modus operandi. People will advance slowly up...He's making me feel like...You're not going to advance two or three levels in a single lifetime. There's just way too much regarding a level, so to speak. And he says, "*Why would you want to do that anyway? Because if it's coming from in here (the heart), you want to feel all this stuff in life as it's happening, so you want to take your time smelling the roses. And you've got to be able to articulate it anyway, so you can't just breeze your way through it, because then you don't know it.*"

From session nine, with Terri K.'s brother:

> He's definitely making me feel like in advancing levels in a physical lifetime, it's not more than one or two if you're going to assign levels at all. And he's saying, *"Having knowledge of the ability of expansion, it doesn't guarantee a swift passage up levels or down levels (however you want to describe it)."* He says it wouldn't matter; you can't run until you walk.

And Gabi's mother in session thirteen:

> She says, *"Some people can make great strides and jump what we would call two or three levels, but it's pretty rare. Most people don't. They get caught up so much in the circus, the merry-go round."* She shows it as a merry-go round.

So...Advancement...Evolution...Expansion. It is happening regardless of where we're living at, be it here or on the Other Side. Moreover, it seems evolution isn't predefined in a step-like pattern, that it is really more of a gradual inclination based on one's own preferences for experiencing reality. Only in retrospect would we label certain periods of existence and place it into a cardboard box and call certain points Level One, Level Two, Level Three, etc. For instance, it's been a gradual advancement from caveman to modern man, but you could see someone chunking out their existence—based on their own criteria—with the caveman portion of the reincarnational self as Level One, and then a more modern tool maker as Level Two. But then again, someone may not parcel out their levels based on technological advancement, but rather spiritual awareness. In that case, the caveman could potentially be more aware spiritually and in-tune at a higher level of advancement, than say a reincarnational self living life in the 1980's. Who makes those determinations? Apparently *you* do.

> "The perception of levels is unique to each individual. There is no predefined a ladder or rungs that you have to traverse—that is all up in the brain."

It is not the point to say, "You will grow; you will advance." No, the point is that you are already doing just that. And that it is okay to take your time; to enjoy the fullness of each and every experience. In the end, Time doesn't matter—only the fullest beauty and awareness of each experience gives us impetus and a natural drive to evolve.

It is the joy of living.

Author's Note: Based on the wording of my questions in this and previous or following chapters, the spirits did answer oftentimes using the term "levels" or "ladder"—but that was for my benefit, politely continuing along a recognizable metaphor so that I could understand based on a limited earthly framework. Hence, I continued to use the term throughout my narrative discussion. But I did not intend for this to be confusing. I want to emphasize to the Reader that most spirits were adamant to point out that our earthly concepts of levels or ladders were not adequate or truly appropriate to describe the real nature of spiritual growth. To leave you with, a better metaphor is that of progression down a highway, an image that a few of the spirits touched upon. Even then, the direction of the highway is not defined, yet may be spread across the landscape, if you will. So, using this metaphor, the states of progression of various souls could be considered to be as if they are spread out along the highway mileposts, filling out the topography of the rich and varied landscape of existence.

21

If There Are No Levels, Then Why Have We Been Taught This Throughout the Centuries; to Believe That Such Striving for Higher Consciousness is Vital? Why Not Simply Live and Indulge Ourselves in the Moment of Life?

When I first devised the questions, I had no idea if there were levels or not, so I figured it would be important to ask a question regarding the absence of such an idea if the previous questions produced exactly that result. At this point, the whole "levels" thing had really been answered, but I still had my sitters ask the question. As always, the sitters' relatives in spirit had some fascinating information to convey.

Why have we been taught throughout the centuries the concept of striving for higher consciousness? A couple of spirits latched onto this when they began their answers. They attached a seriousness surrounding this drive to the belief in the importance of spiritual evolution stemming from religion; though they felt organized religion had actually done more of a disservice by how it was instilled into the overall consciousness of the followers—whether they be Christian, Muslim, Hindu, or whatever, as evidenced by the spirit of Rose in session eleven:

> She went right away to religion. She went right to religion and said, "*This whole concept of trying to strive to be like an angel, that's because of religion. On the earthly plane, that was set up as a construction.*"

Diane from session fourteen broke it down utilizing potent imagery. When she was alive on earth, she never considered herself religious, and this clearly came to the surface by the nature of her response:

> She says part of the reason we were taught that was because we had tyrants—both political and religious—who wanted to control us. She twists me around and wants to put me in ropes, and makes me feel like "*Some of this is just bullshit we've been hammered with for centuries.*" She's making me feel like, in some respect, we want to honor the idea of expansion, but she's making me feel like, the way it was run down here on earth, it was a control thing. "*We need to leave that stuff in the past.*"
>
> She's showing me, the traditional earthly way of growth and expansion, always had to do with honoring and praising somebody else's view of the Other Side and God, and they used that as their control mechanism. It was never about going inward and expanding for the sake of your own soul and your own consciousness; it was always for the sake of another's view of God. That's how the control was done. And she's saying, to actually go out and enjoy life…that was never the traditional way. Should you go out and enjoy life? "*Yes, that's what you're there for, but that's not really how you've constructed things on earth.*"

The spirit of Michael, my first sitter, who also claimed he wasn't religious while alive on earth, declared religion as a major reason why the concept of levels exists. By this time during the sitting, his energy and mannerisms were really coming through, as indicated by the nature of my speech. I personally try to remain reserved while giving information, but by this time, the spirit's energy was firmly saturated in my consciousness:

> He's saying the levels thing in terms of what organized religion has told us is total crap…He's saying don't put it into a religious reverence perspective. He's saying, "*Think of the sun rising every morning. It's something that just is. You don't put major*

religious reverence in the freaking sun rising every day, so don't do this with the whole levels thing. It is what it is, and you will progress, and you will do whatever it is you're supposed to do, don't make it this big huge ritual."

Nevertheless, the drive or inspiration to become greater and greater is something inherent to all of us. This was the overall message from many of the spirits who came through, starting with Jodi's ex-husband from session two:

> He says you already know...the expansion of consciousness. He's making me feel like, everybody knows somewhere inside of themselves, whether it's conscious or unconscious, this portion of our being of experience and expansion. The whole idea of rampantly going out there and doing whatever it is we please, we know somewhere inside of ourselves that's not what it's about. Yes, people will go on these paths, but he says those paths actually in some way contribute to this big balloon expansion.

From Nancy's sister Katie in session three:

> She says the levels thing...what we do to it down here on earth, we make it this big major important thing...She's making me feel like, over there, yes, it's important, but *"We don't put so much weight on it...It's a natural course of evolution...We don't make it this big religious thing."* She says, *"You strive, but you don't make it this big ominous thing...When you make it ominous, you almost make it something impossible to achieve. You don't need to do that—we are all on this road, and this road is all we are and we're just finding our path in who and what we are..."*

One sort of gets the impression from Katie in the above transcript that we need to sort of "lighten up" when it comes to the whole notion of our expansion. Perhaps sometimes we take ourselves too seriously when we finally decide to pay attention and travel the road to greater awareness. Maybe, maybe not? But I do know some people (myself included) who like to scrutinize every little thing we do because we want to make sure it will contribute to a greater good, either for ourselves or for our community. Grace's grandmother from session four contributed this on the subject:

> She says it's an intuitive knowledge in every living thing…this movement …this dwelling on becoming greater than what we feel we are…It's an imperative within us to be that way. She is saying, "*We are bound to this growth that we do; that it's part of the reason we live.*"

From M.G.'s mother in session eight, who echoed a similar philosophy:

> She's making me feel like, "*Striving…because we are aware of what this is, what our purpose is. There's a natural drive to fulfill that. It's just that we've created this idea of levels. We could perceive it another way. But the general idea is there—of expansion.*"

From Kourtnie's father in session twelve:

> He says it's a basic, biological impulse, to express all the energy that your consciousness is. It is like you are this powerhouse of energy and it is your job to fully understand what it is capable of being.

And this little bit from Rose in session eleven:

> She says it's a natural function of life, a function of living. Only we on earth have made it this big awesome to-do list, when it's something that happens naturally. She backs up and says, "*It's like envisioning a plant forcing itself to grow when it would grow naturally even if it didn't prod itself.*"

Terri grinned at the analogy her grandmother used. When I asked why, she said Rose was an avid green thumb throughout her life—a face which I had not known; it would have been exactly how she would have described things.

In addition to the drive of expansion being a natural compulsion, it was also the declaration of most spirits that in order to get the most opportunities at expansion one should indulge oneself firmly in each and every moment. It was an emphatic statement Grace's grandmother told her from session four:

> She says, "*In indulging yourself in the moment of life, that is precisely what you want to do. If you are talking about being a sloth, no, because you won't grow. You will stagnate...*" She says you can't really do that; life doesn't allow you to. You know, you start to feel...stuff...unfulfilled...You have drives, you have ambition...Some people will carry this ambition differently from others...Some people will have lots of ambitions, some people will have little...but there will always be something to move you. Then she backs up and says, "*It's okay to take a rest once in awhile, too.*"

Cynthia's father in session five also spoke of living for the moment:

> He says you should live and indulge in the moment of life; that way you're going to understand the expansion. It's not without carefree moments...But again, he comes back and says, "*The desire is always here, it's an impulse, it's a drive...It's just what we challenge ourselves to do. It's an innate thing in everything, to have this expansion...*" He's calling it, "*growing up...*" Becoming an adult-spiritual-being or something."

Sarah's grandfather in session six describes engaging in life to expand:

> He's saying you are supposed to live and indulge in the moment of life; that's the whole point. That's the only way you can grow and expand...There's an "e-x" word he's trying to say... Okay, he says, "*The only way you can excommunicate false ideas*

and beliefs that are otherwise in your existence is to indulge in the beauty and wonder of life." Now, he jumps back and says, "This doesn't mean abuse with drugs, alcohol, or sex." From his point of view, when it comes to the drugs and alcohol stuff, those people aren't trying to engage in life, they're trying to hide from it. He says, *"It's not that perspective; don't go into that perspective with it, you've got to engage it."* He says, *"You've got to feel like life supports you, that you are safe in life, and that life wants you there—when you feel that way, and you play, it's a party, it's a celebration."*

And Debbie's father echoed:

His point of view, he's like, *"You should live and indulge in the moment of life ... because that is the joy of it all...that is the real secret."* He says when you come from the perspective that you are already at the greatest level (if you're going to assign levels to it)—because Time is a filter that we put in, breathe in and breathe out, breathe in and breathe out—if you can set that aside and understand that it's already completed and live and enjoy knowing that, then screw the levels thing. Don't put yourself in that sphere.

However, there were those spirits who warned about indulging too much, especially without any sort of self-control or requisite knowledge of things. When indulging becomes something more for the ego and not for the wonder and enjoyment of life, this is when things get sticky, as indicated by Rose, who led a rather raucous life while on earth:

She chuckles and says, *"I did indulge—that's what I did. I tried to indulge in the moment of life."* But then she shows me she was unaware of the pitfalls.

Kourtnie's father in session twelve also recounts his past indulgences:

He is backing off and saying, *"Be careful because you might get stuck in your own shit."* He is saying the reason is because back in his youth, he was that other person. *"I was indulging in my own stuff."* And that made him the rough, tough person that he perceived himself being at the time. And it wasn't until he started letting go and seeing how that impacted everybody did he start to change. So he has a different perspective on indulging. He sees it as "indulging" could go way too much into your ego.

However, even if we do get caught up (and occasionally mess up) within the course of our human existence, the events of our lives can still serve in the evolution of our spirits. Remember Brandon who had committed suicide? My sitter's ex-husband who took over answering the questions from Brandon referred to this youth's unfortunate demise and how it was still a point of evolution:

> He's saying our friend over here who shot himself...Doesn't quite understand yet, but he's learning that even that experience produces a little bit more air in his balloon, even though we would perceive it as negative, bad, whatever—it still has its growth potential to it.

I'd like to finish this chapter (and the whole discussion of levels) with a message from Gabi's mother. She encapsulated the whole thing—from levels being simply a perception, to why we should engage fully with life—and why sometimes we go through rough trials. Ultimately, it is the natural process of our advancing awareness. Gabi's mom shared:

> She is equating the levels thing with trying to become all that we can be. She says, *"Because we are driven to become all that we can be, we are so magnificent and so great that we are compelled to explore that; that's our nature, that's what we're here to do."* She is saying, in some ways...She is understanding this in a whole new perspective...In some ways, she intended on having some of the issues in her life she had, in order to go through them...Because it was how she was thinking and how

she was feeling. On some level, she is accepting that she chose having them. She says, "*On some level I knew I was thinking and feeling these things, how I was going to go on down the road.*" She is accepting that.

But the whole levels thing…It's all about becoming all we can be. It's the drive…And you should indulge in the moment of life with that in mind. And then you do have a say. You can influence. She is saying, "*You are looking too much through the sunglasses. When you're here on earth, you have sunglasses on that keep you from seeing the light of everything…*" She is saying the veil is really just sunglasses we are wearing. Sometimes you can pull up a peep and see.

22

For Those Living in the Soul World, Do They Have Constant Access to the Physical World or Do They Have to Be Called or Summoned? If They Have Free Reign, Then is There No Real Sense of Aloneness in the Physical World, or Privacy for That Matter, Such as in Intimate and Personal Matters? Are We Always Being Watched?

Yes! The peeping Tom question! It had to be asked. And it's a viable question. Surely you have wondered about it. As a medium, it is sometimes something you fear, even if only because of the morality behind it. I'll admit, I had an incident of a spirit trying to communicate with me while I was in the shower! Amusingly, it was Diane from session fourteen (before I had done the sittings for this book) who wanted me to communicate to my wife Heidi that she was happy that Heidi was changing departments at the workplace they had both shared. However, that bold communication was really an exception and is not the norm.

Then there is the other extreme. If they are not watching us constantly, how do they make contact with us? How do they know when we are thinking about them? When we call their name, does some metaphorical telephone ring in the spirit world with our name listed on the caller ID? The first answer I received to this question really paved the way:

They can feel you when you think about them, when you start

talking about them. He says similar to the language picture, there's just a knowing. He's saying, *"Getting sucked back, no, that doesn't happen."* He's showing me that they do have the ability to ignore you, even though they are aware of you. He's making me feel like, *"There are people that have been here for so long, that have left people behind like 20 or 30 years or more; they are so accustomed now...Even though there might be people on earth that talk about them, celebrate them, or whatever it is...Yeah, they're happy to get it, but they have no desire to go back to earth and do visitations or make those kinds of connections...They've left that behind; it is out of their consciousness."*

So it seems that the spirits have a higher sensitivity in knowing when someone is thinking or talking about them. However, that doesn't mean they will necessarily respond, given their desires at the time. The answer also demonstrated that if one has been away for awhile, the memory of earth can take a back seat in comparison to the Now moment of a spirit's existence. Here's what Ock had to say in session two:

He's says, *"We are aware of you when you call out to us, but we won't always respond. But that's because where we are, we understand your limitations and your understanding of this (life on the Other Side/Communication)...We will always send you love in return...Whether or not you get it...For some people, it doesn't matter because they understand the greater picture, but you are never ignored. You just may not necessarily be intentioned upon."*

Here, Ock broke it down just a bit further in stating that when we on earth think of our loved ones, they do receive the knowledge of that good will on the Other Side, and the spirits will oftentimes direct a feeling of love in return; however, they won't necessarily go out of their way to make a visit or do much more. That is, they won't "intention" or "force" themselves back into our reality in order to connect with us unless they wish to. Debbie's father in session seven described it like this:

Called or summoned...He says it's their choice if they want to do a visitation. You can't yank them out. They can sense... they have a sense...that tells them. He's making me feel like, *"Do I physically hear you say 'Come here, daddy,'?...No, I don't physically hear you saying that, but I know that's what your intention is, because there's an energy frequency with that, and when that strikes you, you just know that's what is being requested. And so, at that point, you can ride the frequency wave back to the person and interact with that individual."* He says, *"Now there are ways of interacting...It becomes a different form of interaction...we're here and you're there...because there's all this molecular energy variance going on which creates difficulty in getting messages across."*

So, if we take a closer look at this response, we see that the difference in energy frequency from this world to the next does present some challenges in effectively getting things through, in terms of communication. At the very least, it isn't always easy, if I understand what he was getting at. Nonetheless, there is a vibration of energy which the spirits can sense which tells them on the Other Side when someone is thinking or wishing to make contact with them. This sense was echoed again in the next sitting, with M.G.'s mother:

She says they can visit when they want...They don't even have to be called or summoned...She says, *"As long as you are thinking about us, it sends a kind of frequency or note we can pick up on. Now whether or not we choose to respond, that's entirely up to us."* But they are aware of when you are thinking about them and certainly when you are experiencing feelings about them.

And again briefly in session ten, with Marti's mother:

She sets the earth apart from the spiritual realm...And it has to do with energy dynamics. She says, *"The earth sphere has its own level of energy, and over here (on the Other Side) the energy has a different format, different frequency...there is a separation. But we are aware of thoughts and feelings as they come through the energy."* She also says, *"Our lives are here, and like how you can shut us off in your world and not feel us when we're talking, we can do the same to you; but we can hear you better than you can hear us."* And she comes back and says, *"We can come for visits; we can come and not necessarily interact..."* She shows an open doorway..." *We can get things through a doorway to you, but because of the nature of the frequencies, the nature of energy being what it is, it has its limits. There's going to be...portions that contribute to issues, problems, stresses, that make it difficult. Not impossible, but difficult."*

So it seems our calls do not go unnoticed; however, life continues on and the spirits have their own activities which may keep them from answering. Additionally, several went on to describe how access to the earthly realm was handled on the Other Side, which contributes to the quality of communication between the realms:

She says (to me), *"What you're doing right now, with having to alter your consciousness in order to pick up, we have to do the same here. It's not pulling back a veil and it's all accessible, it's a process...it's a process..."*

Here the spirit is referring to the process of mediumship. It is believed that for communication to occur, the spirit must slow down his or her vibrating energy, while the medium speeds his up. When they meet in the middle, their energies are close enough in frequency that the information can be transmitted—much like a radio tuner. Then there are issues with the physical body on earth, which is different than the body in spirit. This creates an even greater challenge when the spirit has been away from earth for awhile:

"If we choose to come, summoning doesn't work—you can call, we'll decide. But when we choose to come, at that point, there's a change of focus we have to do in order to..." She says, *"Remember the communication question and it was an instant*

knowing...When you've been over here and you've got to come back, realize we've been communicating in a different fashion than we used to...And so when we get close to earth and do this sort of thing, we've got to go through...we've got to change things. We've got to do things differently. Your mechanism (body) processes this information differently than we do. So we have to come in and change things in order to...put the square peg into the round hole."

This was talked about again by Grace's grandmother in session four:

She says access to the physical world requires work. She says communication is possible, and the two worlds are interconnected in ways you and I don't understand; but communication is possible...She says, *"In ways, it's like a telephone...You pick up one end here, you pick up one end there...but you got to consider the electronics and stuff going on between the lines."* She says, *"This is what we're working on when we're doing this communication with you...making these electronic metaphors work."* It's not...like the way we communicate here in the physical world where we have physical vibration that moves the air that makes it easy to hear. It's a whole different process to that. She says, *"You may not always pick us up...We're living our lives. Just as sometimes you have your answering machine on and it goes to voicemail, we do the same thing."*

Sarah's grandfather elaborated:

He says, *"We do have the ability to communicate with people on earth, just understand that it is a process...Sometimes it is as simple as whispering in your ear, but it's very rare that that happens, because of the two-way conditions..."* When he says *"conditions"* he means bodily conditions for us...work...He says, *"It doesn't happen very often that way. It's its own process. It's not as easy as talking or whispering."*

But, as stated previously and exemplified here, the difficulties in communication between the dimensions is based largely in part to the dissonance in energy frequencies. And according to Gabi's mother, it appears that some simply do not wish to talk because of these differences:

> She says, "*There are some who refuse to visit because...when you come close to earth, it slows down your energy. Some people don't want to have to deal with that.*"

Of course, time away also contributes to lack of communication—or should I say, a *focus* away from the earth and interest in the spiritual life makes the notion of earthly contact less desirable. Let's face it, if you've been away for several earth years, life in the spiritual world is the norm and earth is just a part of one's past. And in many, if not all cases, that past was not as enjoyable as life in the spirit world, so the desire to return for a visit may not necessarily be strong, as indicated by Jodi's ex-husband, Ock, in session two:

> He says, "*You've got to understand, when you pull away from earth and are over here, like anything, this becomes your daily experience. So, you lose connection with the earth.*" No, no, he has a better reference: "*How often do you go back in your mind and be five-years-old? You don't. You leave that behind as you continue forward. It's the same thing here. Once you get over here, you'll have memories, but you don't keep sticking yourself here to earth.*"

From Grace's grandmother in session four:

> She's making me feel like...the longer you're over there, the less you want to be watching us here. It's a whole new life, new world...She says, "*I'll come watch if you ask me to come watch...but for the most part...*" She knows you take good care of yourself, so she doesn't feel a need to watch over you for security reasons.

Again, the spirits insisted that their lives proceeded into new activities in the spirit world; thus, their preoccupation was not to look back on earth, but to keep moving forward. Diane in session fourteen was quite boisterous about this, especially when it came to being a peeping Tom:

> She laughs and says, "*You must think we have nothing to do over here.*" She says for her, "*I've already lived life on earth, I know what kind of stuff goes on down there, I don't need to peek in. I've already lived it. I know what it's like.*" She says, "*You must think people are really perverted!*" She's like, "*We don't peek in; we are not watching you in that way.*" She says, "*We are intimately aware of what's going on with earth because we are interconnected...In that sense we know...but in terms of spying... We don't have time for that, we are still living our own lives.*"

From Sarah's grandfather in session six:

> He says, "*When you move up here, you have memories of earth, but you can't run back there; you've got to make your life work here, this is where you're at. You're life is forward this way now, not backward. We don't have free access or free reign because that is not where we exist. And there's this innate knowledge that we have to go forward, so we don't keep looking back.*"

From Debbie's father in session seven:

> He says, "*When a person crosses and they get over here to the spirit realm, they are still very much ego-centered and focused on themselves. There's a much greater drive for understanding, for integration, and thus they're not really concerned about earth...The earth-life is done, they just left it; they want to leave it behind, so they're not going to go there, for the most part...This is it. Because we are all connected, there's a spiritual bond between everybody, whether on earth or on the Other Side. When people are in the spirit realm, they are aware of how people are thinking and feeling on earth, if they are open to the awareness.*

*But some people will still be so wrapped up in their own doing,
they will be aware of things on earth, but they will ignore it."*

Kourtnie's father from session twelve added this:

He's saying, "*My God, we have our own lives over here we're
dealing with. I still have that ego part of me…I'm me and I've got
to do my thing. I'm not wasting my time standing around looking
down on you from a cloud."* He says, "*We're not constantly
watching you and dwelling on your life."*

According to Rose, the energy differences do create a sort of filter between the spirit world and us, denoting a form of separation—at least,
that's how she perceived it:

She's making me feel like, "*We are concerned for our own lives, so
we're not living for you. We're still living for us. You're not being
spied on."* She's saying, "*There is enough of a separation with
the filtering that you do have a certain level of privacy."* Even
though communication can take place, even though things can
cross the void, she's making me feel like there's enough filtering
stuff in place that you really can't be a peeping Tom. But she
does point out that everything you do does get recorded
in some way to be played back during the Life Review. She
doesn't understand how that works, just that it does.

From Marti's mother in session ten:

She says, "*The earth sphere is its own place…"* She sets it apart
from the spiritual realm…And it has to do with energy dynamics. "*The earth sphere has its own level of energy, and over here
(on the Other Side) the energy has a different format, different
frequency…there is a separation."*

So it appears there are several factors in place when it comes to communication and visitations from those on the Other Side. Frequencies are

different, and depending on a person's abilities, a spirit may or may not have trouble altering such energies to make communication and acknowledgement, or visitation possible.

When it comes to the sense of being spied on, all the spirits agreed that was not the case. And some of them were really adamant about it, such as Michael from my first session:

> Watched in the physical? He's yelling at me saying, *"You think we have nothing better to do than to watch you?? Hell no! We've got our own lives to live. We understand now why certain things are going on, on the earth; why life works in some of the ways that it does. When we are here, you are there; we don't stand up here, watch you, and say 'Oh, they just f— up.' We don't do that. Yes, on some level, we understand this is probably what we would say if we were there on earth, but we have this totally different perspective now...We see you going through your motions, and those lines of development that you have created. We can't judge that, we don't judge that, because by golly, we did the same thing. So, don't worry about us watching you when it comes to the big peeping Tom in the sky...No, that's not there."*

Since life goes on and there is a new understanding of how life works on earth due to the Life Review (and new residence being taken up on the Other Side), no doubt we are left on earth to be guided mainly by our own means and actions, as indicated throughout the sessions for this question. This doesn't mean we aren't surrounded by spirits—I believe we are—it just means they aren't spying and trying to run the show against our wishes, a notion echoed by Grace's grandmother:

> She makes me feel like you have your privacy. *"We're not up here staring down at you every moment of every day. We've got our own lives to live. We know how you feel about certain things like that, and we have a different perspective of that... And we honor some of those things here...You're not always being watched."*

Sarah's grandfather said it perfectly:

> He laughs heartily and says, *"We're not watching you. We have our own lives to live."* He says, *"We exist, we are alive, we want to keep on living. What fun is it to sit around and watch everybody else live? We have access to the physical realm insofar as the ability to communicate along these lines."*

As I write this, his statement makes me laugh at the thought of people on earth being so glued to "reality TV," such that they pass up their own opportunities for living to instead watch the (oftentimes contrived) lives of others. Kourtnie's father in session twelve continues on the subject:

> He says, *"Personal matters are yours to deal with—nobody is coming in, spying or doing anything."* He's going, *"My God, we have our own lives over here we're dealing with. I still have that ego part of me...I'm me and I've got to do my thing."*

In the end, access to the physical world is there, although it may not necessarily be easy to accomplish nor a desirable act. The beauty and wonder of the Other Side keeps the lives of the spirits in joy and moving forward in their existence; though they do honor us, remember us, and send their love. On occasion, they are willing to make the effort at communication and visitation: drawing near, altering their energy, changing the focus of their consciousness to resonate with ours and the earth. But our intimate and personal matters remain ours—I believe because it is all tied to our personal journeys; they are the lessons we have come to learn, and the spirits know we have to go through those lessons and are unwilling to jeopardize the growth. So rest free—there are no prying eyes from those who have crossed over. Only love, honor, and respect.

23

What is Evil? Are There Negative Aspects That Are as Powerful as the Positive Ones and Can They Have Form and Shape, Such as Demons? If Not, Then Why Do People Experience Such Things? Is It Illusion or Reality?

You really cannot address the nature of spirituality and the afterlife without hitting this topic. Are there bad people in the world? I think all of us would unequivocally say, "YES!" Those who rape, murder, or otherwise cause major trauma in another's life for the sake of their own aggrandizement could be seen as falling into that category. For most, Hitler represents all that which could be seen as evil; for others, Charles Manson, or any host of diabolical serial killers.

So what happens to these people when they die? Do they move on to be like demons we have all seen in medieval Gothic paintings? And what about the demons in those paintings? Medieval man (and many still today) believed that such figures exist. Could those relatives on the Other Side shed some light on the veracity of a hell? Well...Yes. And each of them had a quite a bit to say on the subject.

The crux of the matter centered around how much knowledge an individual had regarding the nature of spirituality and the universe. That is, was someone aware of their interconnectedness to all things? Were they also aware of each soul's unique sense of sovereignty? Compassion? Free will? For some spirits in the Interviews, they did not accept the use of the word *"evil"*—rather, only *"ignorance"*—as was the case with Michael in my first session:

> He says it's not evil—it's knowledge versus ignorance. He says, *"There are just some people who are so goddamn stupid, that they keep themselves down, and they do stupid things."* He says a lot of it has to do with personal power, ego, that sort of stuff, where you have people who refuse to accept their own "sovereignty" and so they act out of their own ignorance, of their own…"precious identity," and so that creates incidents, feelings, or events from these entities that people consider evil.

From Ock in session two:

> He's making me feel like, there is no such thing as evil, but there is stupidity. And it is stupidity that creates…He's saying reference the idea of redneck criminals. You look at the redneck criminals, how they are just stupid, but yet they don't know they're stupid…It's this whole psychosis thing…That's the whole evil thing. It's just people acting and believing and being stupid and not getting out of that limitation and that crutch. He's using the word *"crutch"*…as if for some people they are that way…it's a crutch for them to feel powerful or something. They completely cut themselves off from the greater good.

From Grace's grandmother in session four:

> She shows me…somebody who hasn't grown up and learned their ways yet…They're always in reaction mode—reacting to as opposed to being a part of…They see…Okay…They're in reaction to, they don't acknowledge their connection with; they always see themselves separate from, so they are acting out this behavior, and that creates these events and ideas and things that we perceive as being evil. She says there are some

really bad people here that don't understand that...they are
mentally stupid. Evil is a disconnected person.

Here, based on these previous statements, the spirits are saying evil
people are those who simply have no idea of how connected they are to
everyone and everything, and it is by the very nature of their actions which
reveal this psychosis. As the old saying goes, in hurting another you are
really only hurting yourself, for all things in the universe are connected
and One. There is a lot of scientific data to support this, as tests monitor-
ing heart rate and galvanic skin response of separated couples reveals the
emotional reaction of one does affect the other simultaneously, whether in
the same room or not.

For Sarah's Muslim grandfather, he explained evil people through an
analogy of speed, as if to say a majority of people are progressing along
the evolutionary track going anywhere between 50-60 mph, while those
that are perceived as "bad" or "evil" are moving at a slower pace:

> He says, "If we're going to put speed on evolution, most people
> are evolving at this rate through normal life experiences..."

At this point, I waved my hand through the air to mimic a sense of speed.

> "...where these people, because they are so closed-minded and
> everything, they are moving at a much slower rate." He's making
> me feel like, when you're out in the spirit world, you're looking
> back at these guys, you can't really see them as being evil, you
> can only see them as being less intelligent. Because all of us
> are on this same progression, they are just moving on it much
> more slowly, because they have a lot more issues they're deal-
> ing with, a lot more things they're working out, a lot more...
> He doesn't like the word "demons"...just a lot more division;
> dividing things going on that they are playing with.

For the mother of my eighth sitter, she gave me a wonderful visual to sum
up the knowledge versus ignorance analogy:

When you mention evil, she goes, "*eewwww.*" And then opens up this visual of…of her being up here (like on a mountain) and there's this big gap and there's evil down here (in the valley). She shows me… like mud, muck, shit. She's making me feel like, yes, it exists, but it's very much related to energy…Here's this gap, so it's not something that affects her, but acknowledges that what we would perceive as bad and evil does exist…and she's doing…It's just ignorance, they just haven't figured it out, so they behave in ridiculous ways. She would equate it as having a really bad mental condition. They're like…She is saying, "*stupid little kids, stupid little kids*"…She shows me a playground with little kids tumbling over each other, gnawing on each other, because they just don't understand how to behave and how to interact…"*all these stupid little things they just don't get.*"

Diane in session fourteen really got into the perspective of energy dynamics with this question. What's more, she displayed it in a much larger picture of how evil people fit into the greater scheme of things, a cosmic aspect that we on earth would typically look upon with discontent:

She is saying, "*You have got to understand that consciousness exists in all forms; and those forms you perceive as evil or bad or dark energy, of course are going to exist because consciousness manifests in all these different ways. Bad, evil energy, is just an energy frequency. When you're down on earth, and these people are killing and doing all this stuff to other people, you've got to understand they're not killing anybody since life is eternal, so that's a fallacy. So it's the energy, it is the psychology of the person that is messed up.*" She's saying it's building lessons. In some ways, evil or darkness creates avenues of learning and expression in order for the greater soul to become a greater soul. In that sense, evil has a positive purpose in terms of filling out the knowledge of awareness. She says, "*Even here, there are things we consider gross, disgusting, et cetera; but we have to look at them from the perspective of: this is consciousness in its expansion of understanding All That Is.*"

In other words, according to what the spirits have been saying, "evil" and "bad" are labels we have created which we then attach to certain behaviors that leave us feeling angry, sad, detached, and violated. These are all valid reactions, I believe; however, such behaviors are still considered viable pathways to learning and growth—though we may detest the journey when it unfolds in this manner.

As we learned from the chapters on "levels," what knowledge and wisdom a person has affects what they can and cannot do with themselves; the lifestyle they are able to live. When I say "lifestyle," I don't mean things like who can have a nice car or house, but rather the level of joy or disappointment as accepted within the consciousness of the spirit. At this point, lifestyle and capabilities are wedded together based on a soul's awareness. Whatever the awareness is denotes a certain energy frequency, in terms of consciousness energy.

When we imagine people existing within a frequency, it begins to take on that idea of an evolutionary ladder, where those who are perceived of as having negative behaviors and reactions are stigmatized as "evil." Of course, we all have negative behaviors and reactions, it is just when a person lives their lives primarily from such a limited and life-negating standpoint as a whole that they appear to be in a frequency range we would label as "disturbed." Here's what Marti's mother from session ten had to say about evil people:

> When it comes to evil, she prefers to view it as somebody who is on the lower rung of the energy spectrum. In that sense, she acknowledges evil exists, but wants to apply an energy signature to it. And she says, "*When you're down there in the lower energy spectrum, it indicates that you have certain components of ideas and morals and thought processes...It's like you are ignorant of your possibilities, ignorant of your ramifications; you're ignorant of your energy of how it processes and propagates...Yes, you are the lower rung of the ladder in applying the ladder metaphor. Eventually, you do end up ascending. Evil exists, but it has to do with being devoid of knowledge.*"

Additionally, since the people in a lower frequency range (or band, if you think of it like different radio stations) were considered to be more troubled and challenged by their lack of knowledge and awareness, the reality in which they existed was noted to be a different reality than that of people who were in a different frequency range. That is, if someone was vibrating within a certain frequency range based on their consciousness or spiritual knowledge, their frequency produced a different type of environment and experience than others who had a different vibrating frequency. A straightforward concept, yet so profound.

Let's throw out a visual example. This is completely arbitrary and not concrete. But let's say the type of frequency range a mass murderer or evil sociopath exists at is between 0-2 rungs—this is the rate at which their consciousness vibrates based on their knowledge and experiences. We could contrast that with, say, someone who serves at a food bank, volunteers at a local shelter, or otherwise promotes life versus negating it. Let's say that person vibrates at rungs 8-10 of our hypothetical ladder. According to the spirits, because the vibrating rate is so vastly different from one another based on knowledge and wisdom of experience in engaging universal truth and spirituality, the two do not interact or deal with one another. It is not that the "evil" person is burning or rotting in some torture chamber or "hell," but rather that his experience is far more limiting and does not grant him the far-ranging sight to see from his "bug's eye view," much less interact with, the other reality our "good" person is experiencing from his more expansive "bird's eye view" up on our ladder.

However, since the objective of existence is growth, expansion, and evolution, even "bad" people have the ability to learn, reconcile, and advance—just like everyone else, as indicated by Michael in session one:

> He says, "*lower realm, lower realm,*" so they actually do perceive…I guess this is part of the ladder thing, the different levels. He's saying, "*Partially yes, because they are on a different frequency base, so they would be down here. But as you can see, they can move up, it just takes a bit of a change of will, a change of thought*"…He's making me feel like, this is how you progress up the ladder.

Cynthia's father in session five echoed that view:

> He says the demon thing could be looked at as people down
> here that are of low-level intellect; they just haven't figured it
> out yet. He says, "*They won't stay there. Like everything, this
> innate ability to grow and expand is also in them. They will even-
> tually work out of this process that they're in; they will become
> the angels that everybody else is. They're just...*" He laughs and
> says, "*Just think of them as the snotty-nosed little kids in the park
> that just haven't learned their ways yet.*"

Teri K.'s brother in session nine agreed:

> He's acknowledging these forces, beings, or entities...that do
> exist on this lower energy level, and they do things we label
> as bad, wrong, or evil. There's a "*con*" word he wants to say...
> "*Convict*"? I'm hearing "*con*"...It appears like convicts in a jail
> cell or prison. He's making me feel like, these are the convicts
> that have simply lost touch with the nature of how things are.
> But he also acknowledges, with our life, it eventually goes up,
> so they will eventually come out of their prison and way of be-
> ing and they will ascend...

Kourtnie's father emphasized the soul's creative role in evil:

> He is acknowledging that there are bad people. He says they
> are really dark, if we have to compare them in terms of light
> frequency. They're not kicked down here, like a hell thing. He
> says there is a position of mental wavelength that you cannot
> begin to understand...what these people are going through.
> He says these people are putting themselves through their
> own hell because of their behavior. "*It is the way they perceive
> their energy, so they create this environment for themselves.*"
> They cannot come up here to where he is, because of the

knowledge thing from earlier. He says, "*Creation for a person is concocted by the level of energy that today they exhibit. It will be in accordance with how they're thinking.*" He says evil exists, but the people themselves, are in their own environment, which they create.

And from Gabi's mother in session thirteen:

She says when you get somebody who is diabolical, they are put "*out*"…It has to do with…because of the nature of their energy and how they operate, they are not up "here" energy-wise…She says, "*Because we know we are higher energy beings, this person doesn't have this knowledge and capacity YET…That consciousness…is really all illusion in a sense, but the conscious-ness remains in an energetic state that is equivalent to its 'evil' frequency.*" She says it's on its own frequency /wavelength from others, so they don't interact. She says you have to learn to walk before running, and evil people would be the walkers while everybody else is running."

So it does appear that certain frequencies create a unique environ-ment in comparison to others. How or why this works I do not know, but it makes me think of a quantum leap, where an electron around an atom all of a sudden jumps from one energy state to another. Scientists don't exactly know how or why this happens, but that's the imagery that comes to mind when I think about evil on a series of frequencies or wavelengths. Perhaps new knowledge propels our consciousness into a different vibra-tory state, and hence a quantum leap of the spirit results, thus a change in living environments and capacities as well.

It was noted that those who lived on these "lower realms" were nei-ther imprisoned nor trapped; that spirits from the higher realms would come down to assist these individuals to reconcile their issues and inspire them to advance, as evidenced by these following responses, starting with Ock from session two:

He says there are a few from what we would term the "*higher levels*" who go down to make these people wake up. He says,

"God, I'm glad I'm not one of them." He doesn't think he'd have patience with those people.

From Nancy's sister, Katie, in session three:

> She says there are higher-ups who will go down into these lower realms to try and work with these people and move them into the proper guidance and direction. Then she says, *"Contextual references keep these people from taking the higher road."* It must have everything to do with their psychology and perceptions.

I really like what Gabi's mother had to say about some of these helpers who descended from the higher realms to help:

> She says, *"Those people down there, some of them are really working on their problems and they know why they are there... for a reason..."* She says it is going to be based on their Life Review...They're getting their counseling and healing...But due to the nature of how they feel about themselves and the reality of how they affected people...They have a lot of stuff they have to work out.
>
> She says some of the higher-ups in the spirit guide role were once in these same places. Because they have progressed and did it the hard way, it makes them the perfect teachers for helping people down there.

We have all heard horror stories of people seeing hideous demons—inhuman, ghastly, and nasty. Naturally, I had to include that aspect of this question to see if the spirits really acknowledged such things. To my tremendous surprise, they *did!* But they all said that the hideousness of appearance was an energetic expression of the damaged or tortured spirit. No one mentioned that there were real demons as we have come to believe in them from ancient holy books—no fallen angels, no Lucifer—those are only mythological symbols. No, a "demon" who inhabits the lower frequencies is still an expression of consciousness on the march of evolution; a diamond in the rough that still had its birth as a divine being. Unfortunately, through their ignorance, many souls punish themselves for their horrid, broken perceptions. Not everyone in the lower frequencies looks like a demon—some appear quite "normal." Only those with deep psychological scars choose to appear so ruined—and all for interesting reasons, as explained by the following spirits, starting again with Jodi's ex-husband, Ock:

> He says you'll get people who believe they are so bad or so heinous that they will create this whole facade for themselves. On a serious side, they actually do have mental issues. They do have issues. They're not just playing a game.

From Cynthia's father in session five:

> He says there are those who love to put on the persona of the demon. For some, it's not a joke. They actually perceive themselves this way, partly because they consider themselves defunct or out of balance, or not correct. So, the nature of their energy and belief system surrounding that creates this identity. They are creating an identity. He says, "*Think about the kid that was always put down, chastised, and abused by his parents.*" He says, some of those people over here feel that way about themselves—"*Look how horrible I am; Look how awful I am. I perceive myself like this...*" They have ego issues going on. He says, "*This is all well and good, because there are upstairs people that come down to try and help these people. But until they're willing to accept that, they'll stay where they're at.*"

From Debbie's father in session seven:

> And the thing is, as they...as being so ego-conscious with themselves and not even aware of the bigger picture they are a part of...when they hit the Other Side and get their Life Review...It will freak some of them out, and they will outcast themselves, more or less.

Diane from session fourteen explained it like this:

> She says there are some spirits that will make that appearance
> of being a demon, but there are multiple reasons why...One
> being that the soul on the Other Side believes it is ugly and
> hideous because of the nature of its expression, so it creates
> that image for itself—self-loathing, in that sense. And she says,
> *"Because it's a damaged soul...it's in the lower levels of learn-*
> *ing its lessons, and so it has to build itself up."* I keep seeing the
> word "criteria," as if to say this is something that is embedded
> into mass consciousness because we have accepted it for so
> many millennia in ancient texts...that if you're bad you have to
> look this way and be this way. Since it is imbued in the nature
> of human consciousness, some will simply automatically react
> in that manner because that is what they feel is expected.

Of course, then we wonder: what about people who have experienced
evil, whether it be incarnate, such as at the hands of a murderer, or not
incarnate, such as nasty poltergeist activity? (Not all poltergeists are spirit encounters, but I won't get into that here). According to those on the
Other Side, our experiences are based upon our energies: the thoughts,
feelings, and expectations which we put out into the universe. This will
no doubt be a controversial matter, but the spirits say no one is a victim of
mere happenstance—no matter how it may appear on the surface. When
evil enters into people's lives, something inside the recipient's energy is in
alignment with having the experience (as absurd as that may sound). Am
I saying that millions of people killed in wars, concentration camps, and
wrong-place-at-the-wrong-time scenarios were meant to experience those
events, based on certain energies and frequencies being produced by one's
consciousness? Or those who are victims of other evil doings, such as rape
or incest? Or diabolical haunting activity? As much as I would like to
disbelieve such a notion, that is what those on the Other Side were showing me—and indeed, this does challenge our most sacred ideas of how the
universe works. Then again, quantum physicists have demonstrated that
the universe responds based on the act of observation. That is, it is only by
the act of observation that the multiple probabilities inherent within mat-

ter collapse into a single reality. Who determines that reality? According to quantum physicists, the observer makes the distinction.

Here's what the spirits had to say about those who find themselves within the unfortunate realm of evil deeds, starting with Michael from my first session:

> Why do people experience such things? He says, "*Those that are down there at that level on earth are willing to put themselves in those positions.*" He says, "*You've got to understand, the people who are experiencing the phenomenon are very similar in wavelength—meaning, frequency.*" In its own bizarre way, they've called the action into being. They've called, the perpetrators have responded. There is this interplay of energy going on, from what he's showing me. He says, "*There is no victim. There is no victim.*" He says, these are his words, "*When you're here on earth, you are SO F—— BLIND! YOU ARE SO F—— BLIND!*" He says that's the way it is with the people. When they are experiencing these moments, they are so blind to the nature of their own beingness, that they don't understand how their own consciousness opened up the door, so to speak, to allow this to happen. By the same token, they have the ability of shutting that door as easily as they opened it, but that's where part of the "being blind" comes into play.

Here, Michael expressed with outrage how blind we can be to our own energies and how they can attract and repel the experiences in our lives. What this means is that we may not be consciously aware of participating in those experiences which bring us the tides of woe; that it is not necessarily the intent of our ego-consciousness, but that it is somewhere in our energy, our expectations and beliefs, which can unwittingly throw us into moments of peril. Again, a disturbing thought which we must consider if we are to take a closer look at the components of cause-and-effect, karma, and energy manifestation. Here's what Grace's grandmother from session four had to say:

> She says for the person that is experiencing or being affected

by evil people, they have to have a similarity in place to the
aggressor in terms of energy for this stuff to come together
and interact. She says, "*They may not be consciously aware
of it*"...but she's making me feel like, the person inside, or
some aspect of themselves, is fearing it, calling it, making it
happen, and the energy of the aggressor is aware of it, and
so they come together. She's actually wanting to reference
with something similar to electricity, as if to say, you can see a
natural phenomenon similar to this in the physical world. She
says you can see this in science with certain things.

I believe what Grace's grandmother was trying to convey was the
completion of a circuit, or vibrational entanglement of two quantum
particles. A radio would also be a good analogy. Unless your radio is
calibrated to receive FM signal, you won't be able to get it. Specifically,
station 97.3 can only receive 97.3's transmission; therefore, if we understand
what spirit is telling us regarding bad or negative experiences, our "radio
of consciousness" must be tuned to a certain frequency bandwidth in
order to experience certain conditions or engage with certain other entities
who live and reside along that same continuum. This is not to say that if
you are experiencing evil conditions that you are an evil person, it just
means that your "radio of consciousness" can pick up that frequency
range—that you have tuned your radio to receive it as a form of awareness
and expression in your life. At that point, because you can receive at that
frequency, you will be a vibrational match for others residing along that
same spectrum, and so the two of you may end up coming together, like
magnets, and completing a circuit of experience. Here's what Debbie's
father from session seven had to say:

He says those that are experiencing ghostly type phenomena
that appear evil or malevolent...He's making me feel like,
there could be several different reasons why that is. One is,
the person is attracting that for an experience, and so there is
somebody there willing to play that role. He's saying, there are
some spirits that do have an intrinsic, evil value to themselves,
but he says they won't seek out anybody who doesn't share

or seek out that value system. Those people who have those experiences, in some way or other, are allowing those experiences to happen. He's saying, *"Not only do you have to say you don't believe, you have to feel it."* He says, *"You can say it, but if you don't feel it, if you feel there are still dark forces, then dark forces will be there."*

And Kourtnie's father from session twelve:

They—the people who are experiencing evil conditions—are unaware of what they are doing in terms of knowledge versus ignorance. He's saying, *"position"* and drawing cords. He says people that are experiencing these things on earth in some way are in some kind of resonance with the energy, so it's like some kind of unconscious harmonizing *"agreement."* It's not preplanned, but it's the makeup of energy coming together.

Our science-minded spirit, Diane, from session fourteen, explained it like this:

Seeing demons…and experiencing monsters…She makes me feel like, that's real, in the sense that you have a recipient here on earth who has a fear of such things so they create an energy frequency with that, so the spirits over on the Other Side, who are in alignment with that energy…It gets created. It's a unified frequency. If this person is expecting to perceive something evil and demonic, and you've got this spirit over here on the same frequency…it's going to…it just matches it. She says, perception plays a lot of it. If the frequency of this energy rides on the frequency the earth person is anticipating…She says, there are some spirits that will make that appearance, but there are multiple reasons why…Because some know they can get away with it and the person is expecting to be scared…

If we recall everything else that has been said in this chapter, the idea of an evil-doer and an evil-receiver works in the same fashion; it is an interaction of energy working along some kind of continuum. Diane, as had become her way, went on to describe this outcome in a bigger picture:

> She says…it has everything to do with energy trying to mani-
> fest itself in all its forms and all its properties. She says change
> the notion of a bad "experience" to a bad "expression" and
> you've got it. There are portions of all of us which have been
> murderous and scandalous…Everyone has them, she says…
> because the Oversoul wanted to try them all out. It's the
> big hologram. Then she takes it back to the family thing and
> says now you understand the family relationships…why some
> people don't come back together on the Other Side, just like
> you would not go and mesh with that portion of you that was
> murderous and scandalous, even though you are of the same
> Oversoul. It's all about energy working itself out. She says it's
> all frequency based. Your frequencies…can be different, but
> you all share a template with the Oversoul.

In other words, we are all connected, even to those who we would consider as being evil.

So just what is evil?

According to those who came through in the Interviews, it is a lack of spiritual knowledge and wisdom; it is an ignorance of the ties that bind all living things, usually coupled with a lack of understanding that everything in the universe has a greater purpose and validity, providing immeasurable joy and service. However, evil people are not condemned by a merciless God to torture and pain. On the contrary, they are confined by the nature of their own energy (as we all are), yet not arrested to continue in the march of evolution.

Those who are perceived of as "evil" or "diabolical" are given help in their struggles to learn, grow, and become the divine beings they were birthed to be.

In the field of No-Time, simultaneous reincarnational selves may have already succeeded to the pinnacles of wisdom and will reach "backward" to help the disordered self still trapped by its own shortcomings. Evil, like everything, is a subjective experience, yet certain activities do reflect a type of energy, frequency, and state of mind. It is to this nature of consciousness that evolution is most needed and there are those on higher levels who descend to inspire such change.

But evil cannot perform dastardly deeds without someone who is willing to receive them, whether conscious about that reception or not. Somewhere in a recipient's energy matrix is an acceptance that they can and will experience a heinous event, and therefore leave themselves open to being a participant with the perpetrator.

These are all events, experiences, and dramas, which move and shape our lives through the fabric of Time and Space—with the intuitive understanding that it builds us into becoming wiser spiritual beings beyond the temporal lives we live. It's all about growth and evolution. Sometimes we are aware of the path, sometimes we are not. Sometimes we get so caught up with our illusions, they steal us blind. For some, this blindness can lead to a form of spiritual madness and those who succumb to that psychosis will engage in behaviors without the slightest inkling of the outcomes.

Evil. It is the word "live" spelled backward. It truly is a backward way of being.

Thank goodness we have eternity to work things through.

AFTERWORD

This first volume of *The Afterlife Interviews* has covered quite a bit: the dying process, the new body, communication, the experience of Time, reincarnation, levels, and the nature of evil, just to name a few. At the very least, through the repetitive reinforcement of the fourteen Interviews, we have been witness to a unique form of evidence, which implies that the human personality survives the demise of the physical body at the end of its life on earth. We have been blessed with a glimpse of things to come through the personal stories and perspectives of these spirits and how each has integrated into a new life on the Other Side. What's more, the Interviews have also demonstrated that although a change of scenery can provide new awareness regarding our previous existence, the afterlife doesn't guarantee universal knowledge or wisdom, so our friends and relatives really don't become all-seeing gods peering back at us on earth.

For those who have lost family members and friends, or who feel they are nearing the end of their lives on earth right now, this first volume of

The Afterlife Interviews has hopefully inspired you that perhaps things are not at all bleak. The greatest thing about life is that it never stops living. We can see this all around us in the everyday world. I am reminded of that weed sprout which still manages to push through the cracks in the pavement, rather than succumb to the weight or the darkness. If we take the Interviews at face value, the words from those in the spirit realm reassure us that there is no darkness shrouding us when our time on earth ends. Opening up to the Other Side is a grand celebration; a graduation from all of our earthly experiences, with the promise of more events, expansion, and personal evolution to come.

The other thing this volume has shed light on is that there really is no one on the other side of death's door who is going to judge you and arrest you for bad behavior, though we are held accountable for our actions by the very nature of our own awareness—and that awareness will either help us or hinder us in our march toward progress. However, outside the field of Time, eternity is our best friend; so though we may crawl for what seems like several lifetimes, we can rest assured that we are ultimately complete, and simply have yet to let go and simply turn the key left in the lock to the invisible cell door holding our sense of consciousness captive. At any rate, wherever we exist on the consciousness continuum, untold riches abound and opportunities are everywhere—we just need to be on the lookout for them.

This first volume of *The Afterlife Interviews* has painted the picture of our transition from earth-life to the spirit realm, with a focus on the individual as collated from the combined experiences of the souls who came through the fourteen different sessions. Volume II moves us into a deeper view of the Other Side, where the spirits touch on the actual landscape and environment, societal structure, what they do with their time and how they live a daily life, the meaning and value of religion, how they view God, plus much more. Combined, these two volumes give us a grand picture of what awaits us after life on earth—more so than what has previously been offered, especially since they have been compiled from repeated sittings asking the same direct questions. As I said in the Introduction, if we only had 15% more knowledge of the Other Side, how much could that small percentage change our lives *now* and our world *now*?

I think, greatly.

ACKNOWLEDGEMENTS

To take on this subject matter is no walk in the park. When I set out to do the Interviews, I knew I was tasking myself with trying to bring new answers to age-old questions that had universally been the province of religion and philosophy. No doubt, some of what would be given me from those in spirit would challenge many of the traditional religious and philosophical notions—as well as some even more modern concepts being spoken of in metaphysical communities around the world. In other words, I had to be prepared to face mounds of criticism and heated debate from those with deeply entrenched worldviews. Considering this possibility, I have to acknowledge the courage of each and every one of my sitters who volunteered to be read in order for this information to come out; they were willing to risk their own belief systems and to bear the results of what their individual session would yield when combined into the greater whole. For them to participate in this research, it required much more than the two or three hours of time spent in the course of the reading; they were willing to open up a literal Pandora's box to see just what their friends and relatives in spirit had to say—good or bad. Some had requested their names be kept anonymous in the transcript, which I have obliged, understanding their reasons why. They risked coming forward to go through a controversial process to receive equally controversial answers—yet all in the hope of being able to help humanity in a positive way by revealing information about the end of life and the possibility of a hereafter. To them, I owe them more than just words; for this work could not have happened without their participation. So (leaving last names out for privacy), thank you Leah, Jodi, Nancy, Grace, Cynthia and her husband Shariar, Sarah, Debbie, M.G., Teri K., Marti, Terri, Kourtnie, Gabrielle, and my wife, Heidi.

Of course, along with my sitters came the source of the information that comprised this material—their relatives and friends in spirit. This was by no means an easy ride for them either, I assure you. Practicing as a medium for over twelve years, I can tell you, spirits have to work very hard to maintain a level of energy, focus, and concentration in order to send messages from their environment to the consciousness of the medium. In a few sessions, some of the questions were answered by one relative in spirit, and then the rest were finished by another—no doubt because the amount of concentration and energy left the original communicator drained. However, the commitment from the spirits to answer all fifty-two questions was unstoppable, and so each session thankfully was successful all the way to the end. For those friends and relatives on the Other Side who were able to stick through the whole session all by themselves, I cannot thank them enough for their effort and willingness to go the distance. Every spirit's input amounted to a profound message for each and every question, which often left me stunned and grateful to have been a vessel to receive it. That the spirits were also willing to throw in personal tidbits about their former lives on earth and relationship to my sitter in-between questions to validate my continued connection with them was equally amazing. They showed that they really cared for what we were trying to accomplish and did their absolute best to make sure I was still secure that the connection was strong and could trust the information they were sending me. Additionally, to also expend the energy to produce electronic voice phenomena (EVPs) on my digital recorder during the process—well, that was just icing on the cake. To all those in spirit who came through to answer the questions, I am eternally grateful and look forward to the time when I will someday be in their world and can thank them properly for the time and effort they had expended. To them, I truly am blessed and humbly honored.

Now, any man who steps forward to be this bold (or crazy) has to also acknowledge the love and courage of those who are willing to stand beside him as he risks his mind, his friendships, and his reputation, depending on the outcome of the work. To that, my ultimate love goes out to my wife, Heidi. Not only was she willing to allow me to travel and spend several hours away in order to do each sitting, she also gave me the time and space to transcribe it all, formulate the results, write the book, and then hand it over to her for editing, plus layout and design to make it to final publication. Okay, she likes layout and design; but still, there were many nights she sacrificed to work late on her computer (or giving up her weekends) to facilitate the production and to run the publishing company. She always supported my time to do the work—not to mention the hours afterward to get ready for the book's publicity and promotion (and the stress which accompanied that). My wife has always been my rock and my beacon—without her support, none of this material would have made it to the light of day. She also supported me during those moments when I hit the lowest of my lows (as we all do from time-to-time during the course of a big project).

I am also blessed to be one of the lucky ones whose family doesn't ridicule or judge me for working and exploring the spiritual world. As I meet more and more mediums in my travels, I have come to realize this is a very unique thing. There are so many people out there connecting with spirits who fail to receive support either from their parents, siblings, or spouse; so I am incredibly indebted to my family for their openness and believing in this ability. Again, without their support, I highly doubt I would have even conceived of doing this project. Additionally, what one does not get within the circle of their immediate family, they can certainly find in making new friends who share like-minded ideas and goals. As I continue to go out and offer this work to others, I offer my humblest thanks and gratitude to the members of my development circle, who have become my spiritual family. Without them, I would still be harboring a lot of self-criticism. So thank you Leah, Kiran, Carol, Stacy, Jennifer, Penny, and Heidi—I know I can always count on you guys for clarity, wisdom, and amazing messages from spirit. You are all divine!

Last—and certainly not least—I would like to thank those amazing mediums who not only inspired me to explore a relationship with spirit, but also acted as literal mentors and teachers over the course of my development. Being a part of your classes and seminars gave me the reinforcement I needed to accept this gift and actually own it within myself. I would like to mention you by name, but not sure if I would need some sort of release agreement to do it—but you know who you are! Thank you for bringing this gift to mainstream audiences and blazing a trail for the rest of us—and for giving me the courage to pursue the deepest aspects of it, resulting in this book. Your love and compassion has made a huge difference. Thank you.

> Of course, none of this would have happened without the chance encounter of seven magnificent people when I was fifteen. Your role in this cannot be overstated. Thanks for putting up with my skepticism and sometimes argumentative position. I know I am not the easiest student.

ABOUT the AUTHOR

Jeffrey A. Marks is a spiritual medium and researcher, paranormal investigator, and award-winning author of *Your Magical Soul: How Science and Psychic Phenomena Paint a New Picture of the Self and Reality*. Jeffrey is a compassionate voice for the spirits, and has connected for both individuals and groups in the Pacific Northwest. He is also the co-host of the Internet talk radio show *Explorers of Consciousness*, and is a dynamic educator and speaker on spiritual potential. As a medium, he is known for his humble authenticity, by sitters and spirits alike. Jeffrey is a member and past president of the Washington State Ghost Society. He lives in the Seattle area with his wife and two cats, but you can often find him on the Oregon Coast, contemplating infinity...

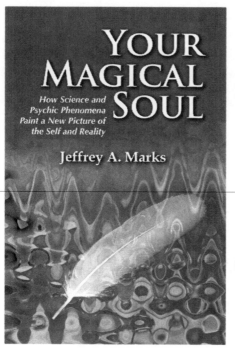

YOUR MAGICAL SOUL: How Science and Psychic Phenomena Paint a New Picture of the Self and Reality

by Jeffrey A. Marks

This award-winning book unlocks the deeper secrets behind what we are, and are capable of, when tapping into our Soul's abilities. Find out how you organize individual and global reality, or how your Soul functions within the context of Time. Casting aside outdated belief systems, *Your Magical Soul* is an intellectual romp by a left-brained skeptical medium and paranormal researcher who takes a tour through his right-brained psychic experiences in combination with an examination of the findings of scientists in the fields of quantum physics and consciousness research to create a new understanding of a very old topic: the Soul.

www.AragoPress.com   ISBN 978-936492-00-8
Available from Amazon.com or BarnesAndNoble.com

Coming soon...

THE AFTERLIFE INTERVIEWS
Volume II

Continue the journey on the Other Side and discover your future reality

Find out about:

The fate of our animal companions
Access to universal knowledge
Soul traveling and environment
Social structure and order on the Other Side
The soul's continuing education
Your spirit guides
The place of earthly religions
If the prophets are waiting for us
The spirits' view of God
The progression of suicides
The concept of a hell

...and much, much more!

ISBN 978-1-936492-09-1
www.AragoPress.com

CPSIA information can be obtained at www.ICGtesting.com
Printed in the USA
BVOW03s1953090514

352690BV00001B/1/P